WELTEN DER PHILOSOPHIE

Gedruckt mit freundlicher Unterstützung der Erzdiözese Freiburg, der Diözese Rottenburg-Stuttgart, des Bistums Hildesheim und des Bistums Augsburg

About this book:
By offering a topical presentation of an unique African philosophical reflection on physical and immaterial reality, Ferdinand Mutaawe Kasozi underscores the relevance of African systems of thought to philosophy.
　　This work could be the desired key to a meeting between the Judeo-Christian modes of thought and the Baganda traditional wisdom, or at least, a significant key to an encounter between Western and African philosophical notions.

The author:
Ferdinand Mutaawe Kasozi studied Philosophy, Theology, Psychology and Social Anthropology. In February 1997 he took his PhD in Philosophy from the Albert-Ludwigs-Universität Freiburg. He now works as a lecturer for Philosophy, Ethics and Human Rights at East Africa's oldest university (Makerere University, Kampala, Uganda).

Ferdinand Mutaawe Kasozi

Introduction to an African Philosophy
The Ntu'ology of the Baganda

WELTEN DER PHILOSOPHIE
5

Wissenschaftlicher Beirat:
Claudia Bickmann, Rolf Elberfeld, Geert Hendrich, Heinz Kimmerle, Kai Kresse, Ram Adhar Mall, Hans-Georg Moeller, Ryôsuke Ohashi, Heiner Roetz, Ulrich Rudolph, Hans Rainer Sepp, Georg Stenger, Franz Martin Wimmer, Günter Wohlfahrt, Ichirô Yamaguchi

Ferdinand Mutaawe Kasozi

Introduction to an African Philosophy

The Ntu'ology of the Baganda

Verlag Karl Alber Freiburg / München

Originalausgabe

© VERLAG KARL ALBER
in der Verlag Herder GmbH, Freiburg im Breisgau 2011
Alle Rechte vorbehalten
www.verlag-alber.de

Satz: SatzWeise, Föhren
Druck und Bindung: AZ Druck und Datentechnik, Kempten

Gedruckt auf alterungsbeständigem Papier (säurefrei)
Printed on acid-free paper
Printed in Germany

ISBN 978-3-495-48236-0

To

My father Peter Claver Wavamunno Kasozi and
My mother Felicitas Regina Nnagawa Kasozi,
Who on the 28th November 2009
Celebrated 50 years in Holy Matrimony

Contents

Preface 13

Aspect 1:
Introducing Baganda Ntu'ology 17

Chapter one:
Introduction 19
Buganda and Baganda 19
Wisdom of the Folk and Philosophy 23

Chapter two:
On Baganda Ntu'ology 25
Ntu'ology: the Etymological Context 25
Baganda Ntu'ology 28
Fundamental Aspects of Baganda Ntu'ology 29

Aspect 2:
Baganda Ntu'ological categorization 31

Chapter three:
Ntu – its nature and entities 33
The Nature of Ntu 33
Entities in Ntu 36
Muntu Category 36
Kintu Category 37
Wantu Category 38
Table 1: Luganda Names of the Calendar Months . . 40
Buntu Category 42

Contents

Chapter four:
Wantu'ology and Kintu'ology 43
Baganda Weltanschauung 43
    An Anthropocentric Weltanschauung 44
    »Spiritistic Reality« or a Religious Perspective of the Universe? 46
    »Stratificational« World View / The Three Worlds 50
Diagram 1: The Pyramidal Strata of Being 52
A Dynamic Universe 53
    »Amaanyi«, the All Reality Permeating Dynamism 54

Aspect 3:
Muntu-centrism in Baganda Ntu'ology 59

Chapter five:
Muntu'ology 61
Muntu: The Human Being 61
»Omubiri«: Beyond the Human Body 62
»Omuzimu«: Is it the Human Soul? 65
An »Integralistic« Conception of Muntu 66

Chapter six:
Muntu knows other »Ntu« 67
Muntu Knows 67
Muntu Acquires Knowledge 70
Proverbs as Compendia of Knowledge 75

Chapter seven:
Buntu'ology 76
Buntu'ology and the Problem of Values 76
Moral Values and Obligations 77
The Ethics of Truth and Falsehood 78
Buntu'ology and the Modality Category 80

Chapter eight:
Muntu-muntu Relationship 82
Muntu, the Relational Being 82
Muntu, the Community Man/Woman 83
The Macro »Bundle« of Relational Beings 84
    »Omuganda«, the Analogy of the Bundle 84

»Oluganda«, the Bundling Principle 85
»Abaganda«, the Material for Bundling 86
»Obuganda«, the Binding Force or System 87
»Emizizo«, the Binding Codes 89

Chapter nine:
Muntu and Deity 91
Relating to »Kyetondeka« 91
Relating to »Katonda« 93
Naming God, Praying to God 94
Katonda! Then, whence Evil? 96

Chapter ten:
Death and Destiny 98
When Muntu Dies … 98
On Death 99
The Afterlife 101
The Foreverness of »Being in Relation to« 102

Aspect 4:
Introducing an African Philosophy? 105

Chapter eleven:
A Discourse on Baganda Ntu'ology 107
Experience: The Source of Baganda Ntu'ology 107
Wonder: The Outset of Baganda Ntu'ological Questioning . . . 109
Doubt: The Rise of Baganda Ntu'ological Critical Views 111
Final Conclusion 112

References 113

Appendix
Epilogue by Professor Dr. Paul Eisenkopf 117

Preface

Baganda *Ntu'ology* is a new term which I am creating, a term that introduces us to the teachings of ancient wise men and women, teachings that are still in use in our days, teachings which guide the present and future generations in discerning qualities and relationships. At the end of this study, we shall pose the question: »Is a discourse on Baganda *Ntu'ology* a philosophy?« This is a question which, as the title – »Introduction to an African Philosophy« – suggests, demands an affirmative answer.

As I endeavour to establish a theoretical base upon which an affirmative answer to the above mentioned question may be grounded, the foremost issue that preoccupies me in this work is whether the corpus of knowledge, naturally acquired and ordered, which manifests itself in the gamut of the Baganda myths, beliefs, customs, taboos, rituals and like practices, etc, is raw material for philosophy. This academic problem falls within a wider context of interrelated questions, the African Philosophy context.

For quite a good number of years, we have witnessed a type of regulated long discussion of the theme, »African Philosophy«, a discussion that has mostly kept attention directed to the question, »Is there an African Philosophy?« It would appear that some scholars are still interested in lengthening this debate in time, extent and scope. Instead of getting involved in prolonging the African Philosophy Debate, it might be a nobler task to subscribe to the efforts that are directed towards establishing certitude about the existence of African Philosophy.[1] This book has, consequently, been written in order to contribute

---

[1] Consider, for instance, the work of Kwame Gekye in which he argues that the situation of philosophy in present-day Africa does not mark the birth of African Philosophy, but rather, the beginning of a new phase of the legacy of African philosophical thought.

to such positive efforts. It may, hence, serve as an addition to the quantum of existing written knowledge on the same subject.

The indefinite article »a« employed in the title of this work to qualify the compound term African philosophy as »*un* African philosophy«, highlights the fact that this study has limitations, especially with respect to its scope. This work cannot encompass all that there is to write about with regard to the philosophical thought of the Baganda. Employing the indefinite article »a« here also points to my contention that a discourse on Baganda Ntu'ology, besides being a search for wisdom, is a part of African Philosophy.

In addition to the limitations mentioned previously, the nature, objective and overall method of my academic efforts in this book set further definite limits. I propose to present the Ntu'ology of the Baganda both in this introductory book as well as in four supplementary works on Muntu'ology, Wantu'ology, Kintu'ology and Buntu'ology. In that sense, this initial book serves only to introduce the key themes of those four main volumes; it thus precedes and leads to the core subject matter of this brand of African Philosophy.

Accordingly, my concern in the present book is to highlight my belief that Baganda Ntu'ology is a variety of African philosophy that indirectly springs from the Ugandan Baganda society in which I grew up, with its religious, social-cultural and other features. At this initial stage of presenting the Ntu'ology of the Baganda, therefore, I am adopting a descriptive format which ought to introduce the reader to the main facets of this variety of African Philosophy. For that reason, the task of familiarizing the reader both with the specific philosophical and related discussions in Baganda Ntu'ology and with a comparativist stance that will search for the broader implications of linking the Ntu'ology of the Baganda with other philosophies[2] is not the key concern of this introductory work but rather a main duty of the subsequent works on Muntu'ology, Wantu'ology, Kintu'ology and Buntu'ology.

Clearly, then, it is not my goal in this book to discern the broad

---

Cf.: Gyekye, K., An Essay on African Philosophical Thought- The Akan Conceptual Scheme, Cambridge, 1987.

[2] Consider S. Gbadegesin's work for an example in that regard: Segun Gbadegesin, African Philosophy – Traditional Yoruba Philosophy and Contemporary African Realities, New York: 1991

sense in which Baganda Ntu'ology as variety of African Philosophy should be categorized. I am, for instance, not dealing with question of whether my presentation of Baganda Ntu'ology is ethnophilosophical, universalist or hermeneutical.[3] Furthermore, I shall preoccupy myself, in the later works but not in this book, both with how my understanding of Baganda Ntu'ology tallies with contemporary endeavours to define African Philosophy[4] and with crucial matters regarding African Philosophy and how those matters relate to Baganda Ntu'ology.[5]

It is against the background of the foregoing explanation on the thematic scope and the related limitations of this introductory work on Baganda Ntu'ology that I have consciously steered clear of the contemporary endeavours to define African Philosophy, endeavours that have resulted from studies and debates on the same matter in the period of time between 1999 and 2010. Nevertheless, the ordinary Baganda Ntu'ological experiences enumerated in this work will later, in my subsequent works on Muntu'ology, Wantu'ology, Kintu'ology and Buntu'ology, lead to philosophical questions and discussions of very diverse kinds.

More to the point, it is a distinctive feature of this study that chapters are grouped into four sections, referred to as »Four Aspects«; namely: Aspect One – Introducing Baganda Ntu'ology; Aspect Two – Baganda Ntu'ological Categorization; Aspect Three – Muntu-Centrism in Baganda Ntu'ology; and Aspect Four – Introducing an African Philosophy?

Additionally, it is worth mentioning that this study is partly a fruit of my two-year-studious inquiry into the legacy of African philosophical thought. It is also the expected consequence of the acts of encouragement and inspiration from colleagues and research friends.

---

[3] Regarding these trends of African Philosophy, see, for instance: Samuel Oluoch Imbo, An Introduction to African Philosophy, Lanham, 1998: pp. 8–46

[4] On the various and varied ways of defining African Philosophy consider: Kwasi Wiredu, »On Defining African Philosophy«, In: Tsenay Serequeberhan, African Philosophy: The Essential Readings, New York, 1991: pp. 87–110; and Joseph I. Omoregbe, Tsenay Serequeberhan, Lucius Outlaw, Henry Olela and Mourad Wahba as they discuss the question »What is African Philosophy?«, in: Emmanuel Chukwudi Eze, African Philosophy: An Anthology, Malden: 1998: pp. 1–55

[5] Among such crucial matters is the question of the existence and conceptions of African philosophy. For example, see Didier N. Kaphagawani, »What is African Philosophy?« in: P. H. Coetzee and A. P. J. Roux: The African Philosophy Reader, London: 1998, pp. 86–98

I owe these women and men of good will a debt of thanks. More so, I am grateful to a friend, Professor Dr. Paul Eisenkopf, who accepted to read through this work. Special credit is due to the Diocesan authorities in the German Dioceses of Freiburg, Rottenburg-Stuttgart, Hildesheim and Augsburg, who financially facilitated the publication of my book. I am also thankful to various authors whose articles and books I consulted during the preparation of this book. I am short of words to express my appreciation to numerous German friends for every sort of assistance that sustained me during the long period of preparing this work. To all of you: my convivial thanks.

Mutaawe Kasozi, Ferdinand
Im Mutterhaus der Barmherzigen Brüder
Montabaur, Germany

Aspect one
Introducing Baganda Ntu'ology

The background of an introductory presentation of the folk wisdom of the Baganda coupled with initial general remarks on philosophy, which are presented in Chapter One below, shall augment my assertion that there is what I term a »Baganda *Ntu'*ology«. In Chapter Two I shall endeavour to explain what »Baganda *Ntu'*ology« is. The first two Chapters will thus offer an outline the key parameters of Baganda Ntu'ology.

Chapter one
Introduction

Besides discussing given aspects of the folk wisdom of the Baganda, I intend, as well, to shed light upon some significant, though non-philosophical issues[1] regarding the Baganda. This chapter is hence an introductory presentation of both: the folk, the Baganda, and their philosophical thought.

The significant, though non-philosophical issues here in question are: a brief word on the region (Buganda) and the people (Baganda); the etymology of the name Baganda; and, the socio-cultural identity of the Baganda. The concluding part of this »Introduction« shall comprise a brief treatment on given fundamental aspects of the philosophical thought of that folk and an operational definition of the term philosophy.

Buganda and Baganda

Baganda are a Bantu[2] ethnic group; they refer to the region they occupy as Buganda, i.e. the southern part of Uganda around the northern shore of Lake Victoria.[3] They are an Eastern Bantu tribe.[4]

---

[1] In taking this so-to-speak non-philosophical point of departure for a philosophical itinerary, I am supported by De Raeymaeker who argues that: »Philosophy depends upon the data of experience to begin its work.« Consider De Raeymaeker, L. Introduction to Philosophy. New York, 1960, p. 18

[2] »The Bantu are a group of people who take their name from the peculiar languages they speak. Their word for people is abantu, hence their name.« See Nevins, A. J. The World Book of Peoples, Huntington, 1973, p. 222

[3] »Buganda ... lies between latitude 2° North of the equator and 1° South of the equator and between longitude 31° and 33° East of Greenwich.« Cf. Kyewalyanga, F. X. Traditional Religion, Customs and Christianity in Uganda. Freiburg im Breisgau, 1976, p. 8

[4] According to A. J. Nevins, »the Bantu are divided into three groups. The Eastern Bantu live in Kenya, Tanzania and Uganda. The Southern Bantu are found in Zambia, Rhode-

We shall later dwell on the fact that most words in Bantu languages are grammatical developments from a particular static root.[5] For the moment it suffices to be guided by the subsequent summary of related words built upon the static root »*ganda*«; they are, moreover, words from which we learn more about the Baganda:

a) Omu*ganda* = a, or one member of the Baganda ethnic group;
b) Aba*ganda* = two, or numerous members of that ethnic group;
c) Bu*ganda* = their homeland which is located in Uganda;
d) Lu*ganda* = their language.

»*Baganda*« is the plural form of the word »*muganda*«. Both terms stem from the word »*omuganda*« meaning »a bundle«, signifying unity, and suggesting a common ancestry, a kinship or a certain degree of blood relationship that binds or ought to bind the Baganda together. This folk employs the same word for »blood relationship« as well as for »their language«; the word being »*oluganda*.« Both blood relationship, be it presupposed or actual, and the language »*oluganda*« are or ought to be key binding elements that fasten the Baganda into a folk, into a bundle *(omuganda)*.

Close in literal and contextual meaning to the English saying, »one by one makes a bundle«, is this related saying of the Baganda: »*Kamu kamu gwe muganda*«[6]. One notes that the word »*muganda*« (bundle) features in this saying. It is a common phenomenon that the word »*muganda*«, its plural form »*baganda*« and/or their correlatives feature in a variety sayings, proverbs, names of persons and places, etc. Consider the following names of villages in Buganda: Kyamaganda, Kagganda; and the following names of persons: Ssemaganda, Nnamaganda, Nnakiganda.

Besides demonstrating that the word »*Baganda*« signifies and/or suggests unity among the members of this folk, we have also attempted to show that this word belongs to the culture of the same people; it is not, so to speak, a foreign word.

Which norm or criterion shall we employ in order to establish the socio-cultural identity of the Baganda? Following C. G. Seligman, I in-

---

sia, Mozambique, South and South-West Africa. The Western Bantu are found in Equatorial Africa, Zaire and Angola.« See Nevins, A. J. op. cit., p. 222
[5] See Chapter One, below.
[6] That is, (collecting) one (stick) by one (you gradually make) a bundle.

tend to adopt the linguistic criterion as the basis of determining the delimitation between the Baganda and other human groupings.[7]

The vernacular of the Baganda is a Bantu[8] language called »*Luganda*.« Besides fulfilling its significant unifying role of linking the Baganda with the other Bantu peoples[9], Luganda displays basic linguistic and/or grammatical traits verifiable in Bantu languages.[10] To mention one example of such traits: most of the words used in these languages bear a static »root«[11]. It is possible, but quite rare that a word consists of only the »root.« The static root is normally a linguistic abbreviation which bears no particular meaning. Accordingly, the meaning of a static root, e.g. the root »*sajja*«, is shaped by use of initial vowels, prefixes, infixes, suffixes, etc.[12]

The Baganda cherish their language, »*oluganda*«[13], as significant a symbol of personal and cultural identity. Hence, it is the fundamental argument of the Baganda that a member of this folk who dearly preserves his or her language, »*oluganda*«, preserves not only this symbol

---

[7] Seligman, C. G. Les Races de L'Afrique. Paris, Payot, 1935, p. 17

[8] At the present juncture, it suffices, to note once again that the Baganda are one of the many Bantu groupings or tribes or peoples. In the subsequent chapter, the third chapter, we shall preoccupy ourselves with additional fundamental issues regarding the Bantu and their languages.

[9] Marsh and Kingsnorth note that, »one link between the Bantu peoples is that of language, for while they speak several hundred languages these are closely related.« See Marsh, Z., and Kingsnorth, G. W. An Introduction to the History of East Africa, London, Cambridge, 1957, p. 3

[10] For instance, Luganda, like any other Bantu language has inflexions with a tendency towards agglutination.

[11] Describing what a »root« in this context signifies, E. O. Ashton and fellow authors have the following to say: the root of a word is the »irreducible element of a word – the primitive radical form without prefix, suffix, or other inflexion, and not admitting of analysis.« Cf. Ashton, E. O., et al. A Luganda Grammar. London, 1954, p. 9

[12] Consider the example of the root »*sajja*«:
a) The *static root* is: »*sajja*«;
b) With the *prefix* »*mu*«: *mu*sajja =[tab]man;
c) Add to that word the *vowel* »*o*«:[tab]omusajja = the or a man;
d) With an *infix*: *ku*sajja*kula* =[tab]to become a man (by age);
e) With a *suffix:* musajjaggere =[tab]a genuine man.

[13] Note that an initial vowel »*o*« has been added to the word »*luganda*.« The meaning of the word has nevertheless not changed.

Aspect one   Introducing Baganda Ntu'ology

of personal and cultural identity, but also the identity itself (the being »*omuganda*«) which that symbol signifies.[14]

This language, »oluganda«, this significant symbol of personal and cultural identity, features in a variety of linguistic forms: proverbs, sayings, anecdotes, fables, songs, riddles, idioms, etc. These forms which »*oluganda*« takes betray not only given socio-cultural and other characteristics that are particular to the Baganda as a people,[15] but they reflect their mind with regard to certain philosophical notions.[16]

More so these linguistic forms of »*oluganda*« inform us: that the Baganda emphasize the supreme value of an ethically good life; that they, as an ethnic entity, have a social structure capable of fulfilling the basic or life needs of its members; and, that they are a people with a long history behind them.[17]

In his book »Ganda Art«, A. M. Lugira refers to Johnston and Seligan, in their work »Races of Africa«, as scholars who describe the

---

[14] So goes the proverb: »*Ozaayanga omubiri n'otazaaya lulimi.*« That is, one may expatriate the body, but not the language.
We may derive the following interpretation from that proverb: a member of this folk, »*omuganda*«, who lives in a foreign land but dearly preserves his or her language, »*oluganda*«, consequently preserves his/her personal and cultural identity.

[15] Way back in 1913, this same point was accentuated in the Luganda Local Journal known as »Munno«: »*Omuganda engeriye ogitegeerera ku lulumi lwe.*« That is, the characteristics of »*omuganda*« are betrayed by his language. See Munno, January 1913, p. 3.

[16] The subsequent major sections of this study, i.e. Aspects Two and Three, presented below, have, among other purposes, the duty substantiate this position.

[17] Take the »historical« overtones of the suffix »*wawu*« for an example of the information that a simple linguistic form can incorporate. This suffix is used, e.g., in the word »*Muganda-wawu*« to mean a genuine »*muganda*«, a so to speak genuine member of this folk. Whichever use it may find, the suffix »*wawu*« embodies the following history. History has it that the interlacustrine region which today is inhabited by the Baganda was for hundreds of years ago the home of scattered clans. Credit has been accorded to the first King (Ssekabaka Kintu) of the Baganda for having brought these disunited clans together into a single tribe. Ssekabaka Kintu is thus said to have crowned this unity-process at *Kiwawu* Hill, near Nnono.
For further information on this matter, see, especially, Nsimbi, B. M. *Amannya Amaganda n'Ennono zaago.* Kampala, 1956, p. 173.
The static linguistic root of the name or the word *Kiwawu* is »*wawu*«. Consequently, this root has been employed as a suffix which is combined with the word »Muganda« to form the compound term »*Muganda-wawu*«, a term meaning a genuine or pure *muganda*, i.e. one whose lineage can be traced back to the ancestors that King Kintu united into one ethnic group.

Baganda as a people with a wide range of variation in physical appearance.[18] I attribute this variation in physical appearance to a variety of factors. Among such factors count historical and political instances that range from migrations[19] to wars, instances which naturally lead to intermarriages and other consequences of socio-cultural cohesion.

Depending upon the preceding observations regarding the language of the Baganda and their physical appearance, I find it in order to think that several fundamental aspects of the philosophical thought of the Baganda, below presented, may be verifiable in other Bantu systems of thought.

Wisdom of the Folk and Philosophy

Earlier on, in the Preface, I specified the key problem of this study and narrowed it down the following question: are the components of the wisdom of the Baganda raw material for philosophy? In this vein, the first task I am confronted with is that of attempting to answer briefly these subordinate questions: what is meant here by »the wisdom of the Baganda«?; and, what is philosophy?

In very general terms, I employ the compound expression »wisdom of the folk«, with respect to the Baganda, to refer to the gamut of the myths, beliefs, customs, taboos, rituals and like practices which govern the various patterns of their life and/or determine their view of the world in general, of the human being and of supra-human beings.

In rather specific terms, I define the wisdom of the Baganda as: »a corpus of knowledge, naturally acquired and ordered, which in guiding and/or determining the life pattern of the Baganda offers fundamental explanations of things.«

The material object of the wisdom of the Baganda consists of the beings and phenomena in the physical, spiritual and supra-spiritual worlds.[20] I shall attempt, in the coming chapter, to substantiate the

---

[18] Cf. Lugira, A. M. Ganda Art. Kampala, 1970, p. 15; see especially Footnote 2.
[19] Consider, for instance, this observation by A. Shorter:
»Among the Bantu there were apparently few clearly defined migrations. … there were a number of discernible points of dispersal.«
See Shorter, A. East African Societies. London, 1974, p. 23
[20] Regarding »the three worlds«, Cf.: Chapter Four, below.

viewpoint that: the formal object of Baganda wisdom or the aspect under which it offers fundamental explanations of things consists, as well, in their religious, anthropocentric and »stratificational« conception of reality and values.

It is basic knowledge among philosophers that the English word philosophy is a compound term and a Greek derivative. Its etymological roots lie in the words »phileo« and »sophia«. The former word indicates an inclination or aspiration or desire towards an object which is yet to be fully possessed. The latter term means wisdom. Accordingly, the term philosophy bears the simple meaning: love of wisdom.

Consider, for instance, W. A. Wallace's definition of philosophy as »the love for wisdom, a type of perfect and even divine knowledge that enables one to judge all things by their ultimate causes.«[21] This definition indicates briefly both the material and formal objects of philosophy. Since it is concerned with everything, the material object of philosophy is »all things«; and, that which this science studies in all things, or in reference to all things, are the ultimate causes of things.

The introductory presentation of the »philosophical thought« of the Baganda and, as well, the introductory remarks on philosophy, given above, comprise an effort to prepare the terrain for introducing my considered position: that there is what I term a »Baganda Ntu'ology.

---

[21] Wallace, W. A. Elements of Philosophy. New York, 1977, p. 3

Chapter two
On Baganda Ntu'ology

What in my phraseology has been termed »Baganda *Ntu'*ology« comprehends three main components; namely, the word Baganda, the basic linguistic root »NTU«, and the Greek term »logos«.

In the preceding chapter, we treated the linguistic context within which the word Baganda falls. In view of achieving terminological clarity with regard to the phrase »Baganda *Ntu'*ology«, I shall now focus attention on an analysis of the two remaining terms, i.e., »NTU« and »ology«.

Ntu'ology: the Etymological Context

As considered in detail above, the Baganda are a Bantu ethnic group. It is also worthwhile to remind ourselves that the Bantu take their name from the languages they speak and that they are bound together as a specific African group of people by linguistic similarities. These linguistic similarities underlie, to a given measure, the socio-cultural identity of the Bantu. This accords the term Bantu specific linguistic significance. It is against the background the linguistic significance of the term Bantu that I shall endeavour to set forth the etymological context of »NTU«.

Following an elaboration by E. O. Ashton and fellow authors on what, in a linguistic context, a root is[1], I illustrate the etymological milieu of the term »NTU« as follows: »NTU is the irreducible element of the significant word Bantu in its various forms[2]. NTU is the hence

---

[1] See Ashton, E. O., et al., op. cit., p. 9
[2] Regarding the variants and meaning of the term Bantu, Alice Werner notes that, the »… word Bantu in its various forms (abantu, batho, ovantu, antu, watu) is the name for ›people‹ …«

the basic linguistic root of the word Bantu and its variants or even its correlatives.«

NTU, as a static root, is such a radical, original or primitive form, which may not be meaningfully analysed without adding to it an initial vowel, prefix, infix, suffix, etc. That is, NTU gains the status of a word only when an affix is attached to it. In other words, the function, meaning and value of the root NTU is modified by adding an affix onto it.

We may therefore classify NTU as a central element of a word, but not as a word itself; after all, without an affix, this pure linguistic abstraction carries more or less no meaning. To explain this state of affairs from a practical point of view, we may note that NTU can hardly be found in the vocabulary of simple, non-scholarly language.

The suffixation of words, language bases or phrases by means of the affix »*ology*« or its variant »*logy*« is a common phenomenon in academic milieus. Consider the following words: theology, biology, missiology, physiology.

Etymologically, the affix »*ology*« or »*logy*«, which in most cases appears as a suffix, derives from the Greek verb »*legein*«, meaning to gather, to say; or from the Greek noun »*logos*«, i.e. a word, speech, reason, discourse, etc.[3] An interpretation of the term, which must have evolved from its etymological background is: *logos* means notion, idea, concept.[4]

Over the centuries, the term *logos* has been employed to encompass several theoretical contexts. Consider these four selected examples:
a) In ancient Greek philosophy, especially among the Stoics, *logos* alludes to reason or even divine wisdom that is the controlling principle in the universe;

Cf. Werner, A. Structure and Relationships of African Languages. London, 1930, p. 17

[3] In the Keysers Lexicon of Foreign Terms we learn more about the Greek origins of this term, and also read the following about the word »logos«: »… sinnvolle Rede, Sinn der (sic.) Rede; logische Aussage, logischer Begriff; der vernünftige, zur Führung bestimmte Seelenteil im Menschen, das männlich-aktive Bewußtseinsprinzip; das ewige Weltgesetz, durch das alles geschieht; das Wort als zwischen Gott und (sic.) Welt vermittelnde Macht.« Cf. von Kienle, R. Keysers Fremwörterlexikon. Heidelberg/München, 1959, p. 234.

The Webster's Dictionary explains this term »logos« is related in etymological meaning to the word »*legend*«. The former derives from the Greek »*legein* to gather, say, *logos* speech, word, reason.« See Webster's New Collegiate Dictionary, Springfield. Massachusetts, 1977, p. 656

[4] Wahrig, G. et al. Deutsches Wörterbuch, 1986, S. 843

b) For many Christian thinkers of the Middle Ages, *logos* refers to the divine wisdom that manifests itself in the creation, government, and redemption of the world;
c) In Christian theology based on the Gospel of John, especially the first Chapter, *logos* refers to divine wisdom; it is also translated as »the Word«, and is identified with the second Person of the Trinity;[5]
d) In some other instances, *logos* refers to mind or spirit.[6]

According to its literal construction, the word »*Ntu'ology*« implies a combined form that embraces the term »NTU« and the suffix »ology«. This is the first and simplest meaning of the word *Ntu'ology*.

In a preceding section of this chapter, I noted that NTU, as a static root, is such a radical, original or primitive form that may not be meaningfully analysed without adding to it an initial vowel, prefix, infix, suffix, etc. Accordingly, to put the question, »what, then, is *Ntu'ology?*« is nearly the same task as to pose this question: what sort of status does the root »NTU« gain when the suffix »ology« is attached to it?

It is my considered position that adding the suffix »ology« to that basic root, accords the root »NTU« a philosophical status. That is, a philosophical term develops out of that combination of terms; namely, the term »*Ntu'*ology«.

The subsequent sections, which mainly concern the compound term »Baganda *Ntu'ology*«, entail, as well, an endeavour to substantiate the philosophical meaning, function, and value that the root NTU gains when modified by the suffix »*ology*«.

---

[5] The preceding three examples, i.e. from ancient Greek philosophy, the Medieval Christian thinkers and Christian theology in general, are also presented by Prof. Gerhard Wahrig and his collaborators in the following summary: »*Logos* ... (Stoiker, Heraklit) Weltvernunft, göttliche (sic.) Vernunft; (Neuplatonismus, Gnosis) Vernunftkraft Gottes als Weltschöpfungskraft; (Christentum) menschgewordenes Wort Gottes, Jesus.« Cf. Wahrig, G. et al. op. cit., S. 843.

[6] Asserting that the etymological roots of the term logic are to be traced in the Greek word *logos*, Arno Anzenbacher also clarifies that »*spirit or mind*« is one of the translations of the word *logos*: »›Logik‹ kommt vom griechischen *logós*, was mit ›Wort‹, ›Vernunft‹ oder ›Geist‹ übersetzt wurde.«
Consider: Anzenbacher, A. Einführung in die Philosophie. Freiburg; Basel; Wien: 1999, S. 193

Aspect one   Introducing Baganda Ntu'ology

Baganda Ntu'ology

Above presented is a description of Ntu'ology from a literal point of view. In the process of describing that term, I noted that adding the suffix »ology« to that basic root, accords the root »NTU« a philosophical status.

My description and/or definition of that term, from a philosophical perspective, is as follows: »Ntu'ology is wisdom that is the ultimate principle for a classification of reality and values according to NTU categories[7].« The basic Ntu'ological methods according to which reality and values are classified are: firstly, analysing and/or interpreting the pattern and properties of the NTU categories; and, secondly, analysing and/or interpreting the inter-relationship between the entities in these NTU categories.

The description and/or definition, above given, should now guide us in establishing what Baganda Ntu'ology is. In the literal sense of the word, Baganda Ntu'ology implies a combined form that embraces the terms Baganda and Ntu'ology. In general terms, Baganda Ntu'ology is (permit it to repeat) a Ntu'ology that manifests itself in the gamut of the Baganda myths, beliefs, customs, taboos, rituals and like practices that govern the various patterns of the life of the Baganda and/or determine their view of the world in general, of the human being and of supra-human beings.

In rather specific terms, Baganda Ntu'ology is: »a distinctive Baganda sphere of Ntu'ological thought.« Firstly, it is a Ntu'ology or a major trend of Ntu'ology[8]. It fulfils all the theoretical requirements for being a Ntu'ology in the sense of the definition given above. Secondly, it is a distinctive sphere of Ntu'ology, in the sense that it is itself an Ntu'ology which manifests itself in the wisdom of the Baganda.[9]

---

[7] On NTU categories, see, for instance, Chapter Two, below.
[8] In holding this position, I feel myself supported by Henri Maurier who argues that the significance of NTU, say in regard to the classification of reality and values is a privileged status enjoyed by all Bantu thought systems. See: Maurier, H. »Do we have an African Philosophy,« in Wright A. R. African Philosophy: An Introduction, Washington D.C., 1974, p. 9
[9] Regarding the wisdom here in question, see Chapter One, above.

Fundamental Aspects of Baganda Ntu'ology

The antecedent description of Ntu'ology highlights the central role which the root NTU plays in the system(s) of thought of the Baganda and other Bantu peoples. Being a basic root, NTU is embraced by, and/or expressed in a series of words in Luganda and other Bantu languages.

Luganda words, words in Bantu languages, or words in general are, in a given sense, an expression of thought or a declaration of the way in which one conceives reality and values[10]. In Luganda a word, especially a substantive, must conform to an underlying form or class[11]. There are over ten grammatical classes in that language.[12] These classes of words, in their turn, must directly or indirectly con-

---

[10] I am employing a different phraseology to refer to the same message conveyed by the two thinkers: Heidegger when he says that, »language already hides in itself a developed way of conceiving«; and Arendt who writes: »language is the medium of thinking.«
Cf. Heidegger, M. Being and Time. New York, 1962, p. 199; and Arendt, H. The Life of the Mind. London, 1978, p. 174, respectively.

[11] Luganda and other Bantu languages do not classify nouns in accordance with a masculine, feminine or neutral grammatical gender. Rather, they group nouns into classes which are distinguished by prefixes. To these prefixes correspond distinctive pronouns. Janheinz Jahn makes this point more evident with the following words: »Es ist wie alle Bantu-Sprachen, eine Klassensprache, das heißt, die Hauptwörter werden nicht wie etwa im Deutschen durch ein grammatikalisches Geschlecht in männliche, weibliche und sächliche Hauptwörter eingeteilt, sondern sie werden in Artformen gruppiert, in Klassen.«
Cf.: Jahn, J. Muntu. Umrisse der neoafrikanischen Kultur. Köln, 1958, S. 104
Dempwolf summarizes these interesting notes on the Bantu classificatory system thus: »Die Gruppe der Bantusprachen in Afrika teilt ihre Substantiva in zahlreiche Klassen ein und kennzeichnet sie durch Präfixe.«
See Dempwolf, O. »Sprachforschung und Mission,« in: Richter, D. J., Hrsg. Das Buch der deutschen Weltmission. Gotha, 1935, S. 152.

[12] Most words in Luganda are compound terms constituted by a singular or plural prefix and a basic root. From the singular or plural prefix, one can always tell the class to which a word belongs. Consider the following elaboration:

Basic root	Singular/plural prefix	Words	Class	Meaning of words
»sajja«	mu- / ba-	Musajja / basajja	Mu-ba	A man / men
»nnyonyi«	Ki- / bi-	Kinnyonyi / binnyonyi	Ki-bi	A bird / birds
»ti«	Mu- / mi-	Muti / miti	Mu-mi	A tree / trees

form to underlying forms, which I may term categories. By a category, I designate a fundamental or ultimate class of entities or of language.

Consequently, Luganda, like any other language, has its own categories which correspond to the Baganda's own view of reality and values. These categories are directly or indirectly based on the root »NTU«; hence the name »NTU categories«.

After thoughtful consideration, I concur with Alexis Kagame's position regarding the four NTU categories, i.e. muNTU, kiNTU, haNTU, kuNTU, which he proposes in his renowned work, »La Philosophie Bantu comparée«.[13] Nevertheless, from the Baganda Ntu'ology perspective and basing myself on Luganda vocabulary, I re-present the names of these categories, thus:

Category 1: MUNTU – the category of existents with human intelligence;
Category 2: KINTU – the category of existents without human intelligence;
Category 3: WANTU – the category of time and space;
Category 4: BUNTU[14] – the modality category.

---

[13] The details about the book are: Kagame, A. La philosophie Bantu comparée. Paris 1976. From the German translation of this work, we read the following about the four NTU categories:
MUntu = Existierendes mit Intelligenz (Mensch);
KIntu = Existierendes ohne Intelligenz (Ding);
HAntu = lokalisierendes Existierendes (Ort, Zeit);
KUntu = modale Existierendes (Art und Weise des Existierenden).« Consider: Kagame, A. (dt. Übers.) Spache und Sein: die Ontologie der Bantu Zentralafrikas. Heidelberg, 1985, S. 106f.

[14] Independent of any written source of information or some other assistance, I have coined the word BUNTU for this category. Its meaning and implications shall be treated upon in Chapter Three, below.

Aspect two
Baganda Ntu'ology Categorization

A detailed analysis of the fundament aspects of Baganda Ntu'ology, i.e. the »NTU« categories, is at this juncture a needed part of this study. The third chapter offers an overview of such an analysis. The subsequent chapter, Chapter Four and two other chapters that indeed do not belong to Aspect Two, i.e. Chapters Five and Seven, are intended to augment that analysis and consequently offer an interpretation of the NTU categories in the light of the nature of the entities in those categories.

In Aspect Two, the second core segment of this work, three terms are brought in a particular academic use. That is, they are employed in their respective contexts from a Baganda Ntu'ological perspective. The three words »spiritistic«, »stratificational« and »attractional« shall therefore bear the meanings which the respective contexts will allow them to carry across to the reader.

Chapter three
Ntu: its nature and entities

NTU is, on the one hand, that which is common to the entities in the MUNTU, KINTU, WANTU and BUNTU categories[1]. On the other hand, however, the fact that there are these four categories is a concrete manifestation of the basic differences within the entities comprising those categories. That there is unity within the NTU categories, is a fact which actuates the analysis of the nature of NTU, given below; and the diversity within those categories is a precedent that justifies that subsequent interpretation of given elements of those categories.

The Nature of Ntu

Janheinz Jahn's summary portrayal of NTU forms the theoretical substructure upon which I may base my analysis of the same issue. Jahn writes: »NTU is the universal force as such, which, however, never occurs apart from its manifestations: MUNTU, KINTU, HANTU, and KUNTU[2]. NTU is being itself, the cosmic universal force ... NTU is what Muntu, Kintu, Hantu and Kuntu have in common ... NTU expresses, not the effect of these forces, but their being. But the forces act continually and are constantly effective. Only if one could call a halt to the whole universe, if life suddenly stood still, would NTU be revealed.«[3]

Jahn's fore-going analysis is certainly a credit to the understanding of NTU; it highlights the link between the ontological notion of

---
[1] Reference is hereby made to the four principal Ntu categories in Baganda Ntu'ology, categories expounded in the fore-going Chapter.
[2] One is hereby reminded that J. Jahn adopts the presentation of the NTU by Alexis Kagame, referred to in Chapter Two, above. While A. Kagame employs *Kinyarwanda*, I use Luganda to address the same issue; both are Bantu languages, after all.
[3] Jahn, J. Muntu. The new African Culture. New York, 1961, p. 101

being and NTU. It is an observation worthy point that Jahn's basic premise upon which he establishes the above presented explanation is the following one: »NTU is being itself; NTU is the cosmic force.« There is a strong likelihood that Janheinz Jahn borrows this identification of being with force, and eventually with NTU, from Placide Tempels[4]. Tempels is moreover a scholar whose work on Bantu systems of thought preoccupies Jahn a great deal[5].

Jahn's above-given basic premise, with its consequent identification of being with force and eventually with NTU, deserves the following notes of correction[6]. Firstly, the identification of being with force is not in harmony with Baganda Ntu'ology. To what effect may we, then, analyse NTU against the foundation of a false basic premise?

Secondly, NTU is exclusively »closely linked with being itself,« it is not being itself. Thirdly, NTU, as we shall learn in more detail later, entails a force; it is itself not a force, however. Fourthly, presuming that Jahn intends to mean by »being itself« the Absolute Being, then this equation, too, is incompatible with Baganda Ntu'ology. The Absolute Being supersedes the levels of the NTU categories.[7] In which manner may we, then, conceive of identifying the former with the latter?

The antecedent notes of correction present more information about »what NTU is not«, than about »what NTU is«. It is then imperative to offer some positive observations about the nature of NTU. The key apothegm in this section runs thus: NTU is that which is common to the entities in the MUNTU, KINTU, WANTU and BUNTU categories. The obvious implication of this literal formulation is that all forms of reality and values encompassed in the above mentioned

---

[4] Placide Tempels maintains that for the Bantu as well as for all Africans, being is force and force is being.
Cf. Tempels, P. Bantu Philosophy. Paris, 1959, p. 35
[5] Besides his preoccupation with Tempels' work, Jahn even attempts to forge a synthesis out of that work and Alexis Kagame's work on language and being (referred to in Chapter Two). So writes Heinz Kimmerle with regard to that matter: »J. Jahn versucht eine Synthese aus Tempels' und Kagames Werk, bei der aber die inneren Spannungen zwischen beiden übersehen werden.«
See Kimmerle, H. Philosophie in Afrika – afrikanische Philosophie. Frankfurt a. M., 1999, p. 37, footnote 8.
[6] We shall revisit these points of correction in a more positive manner, either in the subsequent paragraphs of this chapter, or in the next chapter.
[7] Consider Chapter Four below, for further information on this matter.

categories bear some reference to NTU. This implies further that NTU is very closed linked with being itself. It is not, nonetheless, being itself.

All existents partake of the basic elements of being. Accordingly, NTU, being that which is common to all existents in the above-given four categories, includes in its nature a dynamism which urges all such existents to the fundamental elements of being. NTU qualifies, hence, for that principle which acts as a synthesizing dynamic factor that pervades all such existents. Since an element which is common to and similar in all entities in the above given categories is embedded in its nature, NTU is also an all-embracing principle.

The peculiar advantage of being the most primitive and most irreducible of all roots in Luganda and other Bantu languages was assigned NTU in the previous Chapter. Every other basic root in Luganda may ultimately be reduced to one of the NTU categories. The root NTU, nevertheless, may not and cannot be reduced to any other form. With this root we come to, so to say, a standstill.[8] Consider the following examples: ki*swa* (ant hill), mu*ti* (tree), ma*kubo* (roads). In each of these instances, the ending written in italics, is the basic root of that word. It is a note worthy point that these roots, which admit of no further analysis of themselves, can singly or generally, be reduced to the NTU category of »existents without human intelligence,« the KINTU category. KINTU itself, like the other three categories is reducible to NTU.

Among the linguistic basic roots in Luganda, NTU enjoys the widest extension. This is so since its categories, regarded in their totality, envelop almost all reality and values. There is no other basic root in Luganda that defies NTU in this regard.

If we blend the last two observations about this basic root, we may correctly conclude that NTU is the instance of coalescence, the point of juncture of all roots in Luganda. It is thus an expression of the coalescence of varied modes of being. It is in this regard that we consider NTU to be »closely linked with being itself.« It is, however, important to reiterate the observation that NTU is exclusively »closely linked with being itself,« it is not being itself.

---

[8] By »coming to a standstill«, I do not mean the same thing as Janheinz Jahn does when, in his above quoted analysis, he writes that, »only if one could call a halt to the whole universe, if life suddenly stood still, would NTU be revealed.« See Jahn, J. op. cit., p. 101. I shall, moreover, later assert that NTU has no ontological status; it cannot, hence, be something, like Jahn puts, it that is to be revealed when the whole universe has been called to a halt.

If NTU, like we have said over again, is barely »closely linked with being itself« and that it is not being itself, what is it then? Although NTU is that which is common to the entities in the MUNTU, KINTU, WANTU and BUNTU categories, it remains the product of a series of linguistic reductions. These linguistic reductions entail the loss of the significant, specific or particular characteristics of the word being reduced to its primitive form, to the effect that what remains behind as a root is but the indeterminate original form of that word.[9] Accordingly, NTU may not be conceived to be being itself or a reality with a distinct ontological status independent of the mind. In the subsequent sections of this study, we shall consider in more detail that NTU is a logical reality which has no existence of its own independent of that given to it by the mind. It is, after all, what I termed a linguistic reduction. It is an abstracted term which, as a consequence of being what it is, cannot enjoy extra-mental existence.

Following Henri Maurier, we may further describe NTU as a term expressing an idea, an intuition of the real, an intuition of the core of being.[10]

Entities in Ntu

Let us revisit the key apothegm in this section which runs thus: NTU is that which is common to the entities in the MUNTU, KINTU, WANTU and BUNTU categories. Following the counsel of this apothegm, one notes that most modes of being may be classified under these NTU categories. These categories constitute what I may name »the system of Baganda Ntu'ological Categorization« of reality and values. What are the entities embraced by each of these categories?

Muntu Category

The Luganda word »*Muntu*« (plural: »*Bantu*«) means human being. Named after this word, is the category of existents with human intelli-

---

[9] In Chapter Two we learnt that such a radical form of a word may not be meaningfully analysed without adding to it an initial vowel, prefix, infix, suffix, etc.
[10] Maurier, H. op. cit., p. 9

gence *(amagezi)*. Besides intelligence, entities in this category are endowed with the capacity to speak *(okwogera)*; this capacity is another qualifying characteristic for adhering to this category. As much as I know, it is only human beings who fulfil these two conditions; no wonder, then, that they alone constitute this category.

Kintu Category

The Luganda word »*Kintu*« (plural: »*Bintu*«) means thing, object. Named after this word, is the category of existents without human intelligence. The entities in this category include all spiritual beings, for instance, the gods *(balubaale)*, the spirits *(mizimu)*, etc. The rest of the physical beings that do not belong to the Muntu category are also counted among the constituent entities of this group.

Among the *BINTU*, i.e. the entities in the *KINTU* category, there is the class of »*BINTU*« which are superior to the »*MUNTU*«, the human being; and, then, the class of things that are inferior to the human being. The former is the class of spiritual beings; let us call them »the spiritual *Bintu*«; and the latter, that of physical beings we may name them »the physical *Bintu*«.

In Baganda Ntu'ology, the spiritual Bintu hold the mode of existence between the Absolute Being and the human beings[11]. The entire existence of muntu, the human being, is naturally ordained to have its ultimate end in the spiritual Bintu class of the KINTU category. The spiritual Bintu comprise, so to speak, the ontological destiny of muntu, the human being. After his/her death, Muntu the human being, has to be associated with one of the four types of spiritual beings[12], beings that are indeed entities in the KINTU category.

In the realm of material beings[13], *muntu*, the human being is deemed to be the acme of natural reality. In constituting the ontological

---

[11] The next Chapter shall furnish us with a more elaborate consideration of the stratification of the varied and various modes of existence according to Baganda Ntu'ology.

[12] The four types of spiritual beings here in question, in singular / plural forms respectively, are: *muzimu / mizimu; jjembe / mayembe; musambwa / misambwa;* and *lubaale / balubaale*. The meaning of these terms shall become elaborate in the later sections of this study, especially in Chapters Four, Five and Ten, below.

[13] Included in this realm of material beings are both human beings (Muntu category) and physical beings (Kintu category).

destiny of *muntu*, who is the acme of natural reality, the spiritual *Bintu* qualify for the highest aspiration of all natural reality, the zenith of natural reality.

The group of the physical *bintu* embraces any type of material things which do not belong to the MUNTU category. Treating the hierarchy of being in Baganda Ntu'ology in the next chapter, I attempt to demonstrate the point that: while the spiritual *Bintu* comprise, so to speak, the ontological destiny of muntu, the human being, the physical *Bintu* must succumb to the superiority of *muntu*, the human being.

In regard to the superiority of the human being over the physical beings, the Baganda and the protagonists of the Judeo-Christian tradition appear to hold the same position. That is, the stand point that the human being has to subdue the rest of the physical beings and even use them for his/her purposes.[14]

The physical *Bintu*, according to Baganda Ntu'ology, also serve as a base from which the human being journeys towards his ontological destiny. They are as well his/her instruments, tools, »servants« in day-to-day life.

Following from the above said, *muntu*, the human being is the binding element between the spiritual and the physical beings, i.e. between the two classes of entities in the KINTU category. That means, in the hierarchy of being, *muntu*, the human being, is the dividing line between the two classes; the human being remains the uniting link between the two, however.

Wantu Category

The Luganda word »*Wantu*« means »a certain place«, »somewhere«, or »space in general«. Another Luganda rendering the meaning of the English term or notion »space« is »*bbanga*«. In addition to the connotation of space that surrounds the word »*bbanga*« is this alternative meaning: »*bbanga*« is as well »time«, »interval«. In the instance where one speaks about »*(e)bbanga (e)ggwanvu*«, there is a double message that one communicates by the use of the term »*bbanga*«. That phrase could refer either to »a long period of time, a long interval«, or to »a long distance, gap.«

---

[14] See also Judeo-Christian Book of Genesis, Chapter 1, verses 27–30

*Where*ness, *somewhere*ness, *when*ness are therefore key characteristic elements of the WANTU category.

It is a worthy noting point that the Absolute Being too, despite the strong likelihood that he is inexpressible in any of the NTU categories, is to a given extent enveloped in the WANTU category. His abode, like his name is *»ggulu«*, i.e. the sky or the heavens. That means, the Absolute Being is somewhere.

It follows from the above said that, in Baganda Ntu'ology the notions of space and time stand in a closely related similarity of meaning. It is no wonder, then, that the two entities, space and time, are components of the same NTU category, the *WA*NTU category.

A characteristic common to both time and space is, to put it plainly, »occupiedness« or the emptiness deficiency. That is, in Baganda Ntu'ology, neither of the two entities is considered as devoid of contents. Discussing the dynamic conception of the universe in the next chapter[15], we shall note that the Baganda conceive of the universe as filled up with a certain dynamism. It is in this vein that space can hardly be viewed as a vacuum.

Similar to space, time, too, is apprehended as being inhabited by a type of dynamism; time is perceived in relation to events. Time is, hence, never empty. For instance, there many instances of names of individual persons that facilitate in recalling when, at what time, under what historical circumstances that individual was born. Take the example of the name *»Zaavuga«* (i.e., they sounded, meaning: there was gun fire); or the name *»Ziriddamu«* (i.e., fighting will resume). A person bearing such a name is, in most of the cases, one who was born in times of war.

Let us consider yet another example: the shaking or trembling of the earth, may be marked by assigning the name *»Musisi«* (earthquake) to a child born around the time of the happening of that event. Surviving death in war, shipwreck, landslide, etc. may earn one the name *»Kawonawo«* (survivor).

In Baganda Ntu'ology, even the future is not empty. It is also filled up with forces and events. It would appear, the Baganda hold a predeterministic view of the future. That is, the future events in an individual's life are ordained for him/her beforehand; he/she just cooperates with this predetermined future as it unravels itself into the pre-

---

[15] Cf. The section on »a dynamic universe« in Chapter Four, below.

Aspect two   Baganda Ntu'ology Categorization

sent. A common personal name expressing hope in the coming times is »*Tusuubira*« (we hope).

The historical happening of certain events is also kept in mind by assigning names to places where such events occurred. E.g. the name »*Kiteezi*«, a village in Kyaddondo County in Buganda, reminds the residents of that village of the long past days of insecurity, when »malicious robbers and thugs« (i.e. *abateezi abalina ettima*) used to launch surprise attacks on travellers at a road point in that village.

The »occupiedness« of, or the emptiness deficiency in the entity time may also be expressed in compound names assigned to eras or epochs in the history of the Baganda. For instance, »*emirembe emikabya*« means »the era or reign of King Muteesa the terrible«. One may thus say, my grandfather flourished in the »*emirembe emikabya*«, during the reign of Muteesa I.

A word on the names given to the months of the calendar year may likewise substantiate the argument for the occupiedness of time or the emptiness deficiency in the entity time. As the Table below shows, these names are based on the key events in the annual agricultural cycle of life in the Lake Victoria shore region called Buganda.

Table 1 Luganda Names of the Calendar Months

Month	Event	Luganda Name	Meaning of the name
January	ripening of bananas due to the dry season	GATONNYA	they (bananas) are dropping down
February	dry season causes dry-ness of banana leaves	MUKUTULA-NSANJASANJA	that (heat) which ›cuts‹ dried banana leaves down from the stem
March	the rainy season begins	MUGULA-NSIGO	that period in which seeds are bought
April	there are lots of white ants named »mpawu«	KAFUMUULA-MPAWU	that period in which »mpawu« fly

Month	Event	Luganda Name	Meaning of the name
May	peak of the rainy season; crops appear to be full of sap	MUZIGO	oil; i.e., the vegetation looks as if it were smeared with oil
June	many cases of fever	SSEBO-ASEKA	»father is smiling« (so thinks the child; but he is actually dead due to fever)
July	a lot of farm or garden activities	KASAMBULA	that period in which fields are cleared
August	another rainy season begins; for Baganda, a new year begins	MUWAKANYA	the opposing season – it is »obstructing« the old year / season
September	selling farm products	MUTUNDA	that period in which garden products are sold
October	heavy rain falls	MUKULUKUSA-BITUNGOTUNGO	the period of the rains which erode the simsim seedlings
November	presence of a lot of grasshoppers	MUSEENENE	the season of grasshoppers (nseenene)
December	presence of a lot of insects named »ntenvu«	NTENVU	Insects called »ntenvu«

The fore-going arguments for what I have called the occupiedness of, or the emptiness, deficiency in the WANTU entities of space and time, justify the position that WANTU is that wherein reality and values are contained. The elements »whereness,« »somewhereness« and »whenness« can be directly or indirectly applied to the whole of reality and values. Hence, the WANTU category embraces, envelopes all the other categories and the entities therein.

Aspect two Baganda Ntu'ology Categorization

Buntu Category

»*Buntu*« is a word I coined for this category. What, then, does this term mean? The Luganda word »*Buntu*« means tiny, small things, objects. Named after this word is, however, not the category of tiny things or objects, but rather the modality category. One observes that most words in Luganda which are employed to express the modality of things and values begin with the prefix »BU«. I have therefore coined the term »BUNTU« out of the combination of the prefix BU and the static root NTU.

The entities in this category are therefore provisions regarding the measure, manner, procedure, form, variety, expression, manifestation, arrangement and pattern of being and values. Such provisions concern a variety of themes regarding the modality of being and values, for instance, the themes: education, aesthetic values, freedom, responsibility, virtues, vices, norms, knowledge, weights, measures, health, character traits, etc. Later sections of this study, especially Chapter Seven, shall highlight these instances in more detail.

Chapter four
Wantu'ology and Kintu'ology

The Baganda »Weltanschauung« and the view of the same folk about a universe permeated with a dynamic power are the key themes in this section, a section where I present yet two new terms, namely, »Wantu'ology« and »Kintu'ology«.

By »Wantu'ology« and »Kintu'ology«, I cite two separate but interdependent sub-divisions of Baganda Ntu'ology. I am thus employing these two terms to allude to wisdom that is the basic principle for a classification of reality and values according to *Wantu* and *Kintu* categories of being, respectively. In this vein, I shall accord special attention to analysing and/or interpreting the inter-relationship between the entities in these two NTU categories. I shall as well attempt to treat along the same lines the inter-relationship between entities in these categories and the rest of reality and values.

Baganda Weltanschauung

The German substantive »*Weltanschauung*« is employed here against the background of its literal meaning; that is, »*Weltanschauung*« as referring to the manner in which one perceives and interprets the world.[1] In this sense of the word, I shall endeavour to demonstrate that the Baganda Weltanschauung consists in an anthropocentric, »religio-spiritistic« and »stratificational« world view. I shall also maintain that world for the Baganda is a contingent world.

---

[1] I am describing this term along the lines of its dictionary meaning, i.e. die »Art und (sic.) Weise, wie jemand (sic.) die Welt und (sic.) ihren Sinn sowie sein Dasein in ihr betrachtet und beurteilt.«
Cf. Wahrig, G. et al. op.cit., p. 1425.

Aspect two   Baganda Ntu'ology Categorization

An Anthropocentric Weltanschauung

In his »Introduction to African Religion,« John Samuel Mbiti highlights a view prevailing among several African peoples according to which the human being is the most important entity of the universe.[2] Regarding himself or herself as being so important, the human being consequently tends to interpret the world in terms of human experience and values. In the subsequent paragraphs of this sub-section, I shall argue that the Baganda, too, hold this world outlook which I have named »an anthropocentric[3] Weltanschauung.«

Treating the idea of the universe as a »spiritistic« reality, we shall soon assert that the Baganda hold a vague idea of the creation of the world. Underlying the idea of a created world is the notion of a creator. It is worth noting that there is very little elaboration on this creator in the gamut of the myths, beliefs, customs, taboos, rituals and like practices which govern the various patterns of the life of the Baganda and/or determine their view of the world in general, of the human being and of super-human beings. In the absence of such elaborations on a creator of the universe, we are inclined to conclude that the Baganda conceive of the Absolute Being as a creator in order to establish a basis for explaining their own existence and their own environment. In other words, among the Baganda, the purpose of the notion of a creator is to explain the origin of the human being and other things that serve his/her sustenance. The conception of a creator is hence a point on the list of my arguments for their anthropocentric Weltanschauung.

That the human being is held by the Baganda to be the centre of the universe is substantiated further by their view concerning the superiority of the human being over the physical beings. Expressions of Baganda wisdom, like the saying, »*ekitayogera tekirema ayogera*,«[4] bolster the stand point that the human being has to subdue the rest of the physical beings and even use them for his/her purposes. Therefore,

---

[2] Reference is made to: Mbiti, J. S. Introduction to African Religion. London, 1978, pp. 37–38. Mbiti's work, here quoted, shall henceforth be referred to as: »Mbiti, J. S. Introduction«.

[3] The Greek words underlying this term are: »*Anthropos*« meaning human being; and »*kentron*« *that* is centre.

[4] Id est, »the human being, who is endowed with the ability to speak (the human being) cannot fail to subdue a being which cannot express thoughts, feelings or opinions orally.«

the physical beings of the Kintu category or the physical *bintu* exist with the sole, final purpose of serving the existence of the human being.

Considered from the view point of the spiritual beings of the Kintu category or the spiritual *bintu*, the human being stands once again at the centre of, so to say, the parade of physical and spiritual beings. In the hierarchy of beings, treated below, the human being plays an intermediary role of bridging the physical and the spiritual worlds. He/she is the point of contact and communication between the two worlds.

Furthermore, in the hierarchy of beings, treated below, the spiritual beings possess, on the one hand, a more elevated position than the human beings. On the other hand, however, the same spiritual beings, viewed with an anthropocentric eye, serve the purpose of explaining the destiny of the human being.[5]

By means of expressions like the saying presented earlier, i.e. »*ekitayogera tekirema ayogera*«, the human being declares his/her capacity for self-reflection and consciousness as expressed in the language of the spoken word. In the above given instance, the human being experiences himself/herself as a being that knows something about its capacities and capabilities and, as well, as a being that knows something concerning the inabilities of the physical beings. This self-experience is typically anthropocentric in two senses: firstly, the superiority of the human being over physical beings of the Kintu category is emphasized thereby; and, secondly, the human being presents himself/herself as the knower, the subject, while the other beings are the known, the objects.

Earlier on I stated that: in asserting his/her superiority over the other physical beings, the human being puts the latter into its service. The physical beings of the Kintu category or the physical bintu are hence valuable and significant to the existence of the human being. Their being »valuable and significant to the existence of the human being« earns them accidental qualities or attributes. Accordingly, in Baganda Ntu'ology, an attribute of a physical being depends upon the value and significance of that single being to the human being.

Following from the antecedent elaboration, attributes of being in Baganda Ntu'ology are human-being-relative, they are extrinsic, and

---

[5] Like we stated in Chapter Three above, the spiritual beings or spiritual bintu comprise the ontological destiny of the human being.

they are anthropological.[6] Perceived from the angle of »attributes of being«, reality, to include both spiritual and physical beings[7], forms three categories which I assign the following descriptive names:
i. The category of security, which incorporates beings that are serviceable, valuable, beneficial, etc. to the human being;
ii. The category of precariousness, which embodies beings that are hazardous, harmful, etc. to the human being;
iii. The category of neutrality, which encompasses beings that are indifferently disposed to the human being.

The Baganda world view is not only positively anthropocentric. Rather, its anthropocentrism bears negative overtones as well. Consider for instance, the stand-point that the human being is also responsible for much of the catastrophes and disorders in the universe.[8]

Besides demonstrating the anthropocentrism prevailing in the Baganda Weltanschauung, I have also touched upon the point that: in the mind of these people, the universe is not barely a stage of natural things and events, but more so a cultural world, a world of interactions of beings.

»Spiritistic Reality« or a Religious Perspective of the Universe?

Is the world in which the Baganda live spiritistic, or do they perceive the world from a fundamentally religious perspective?

I concur with John Samuel Mbiti's position about the religiosity of African peoples to assert that the Baganda, like the other Africans, are

---

[6] This description calls to mind a comparison or even a contrast of this view point with the Western Philosophy perspective in regard to the attributes of being. For instance, the transcendental attributes: ontological truth, ontological goodness, ontological unity.
[7] Despite the fact that I have treated only the physical beings in the fore-going brief elaboration on the attributes of being, I have chosen to introduce the spiritual beings into the current discussion, since what has been said about the former applies mutatis mutandis to latter. After all, the spiritual beings, viewed with an anthropocentric eye, serve the purpose of explaining the destiny of the human being. They, like the physical beings, are assessed or appreciated according to the way in which they are »valuable and significant to the existence of the human being«; and this earns them accidental qualities or attributes.
[8] We shall revisit this question of the human being bearing due responsibility for the disorder in the universe in Chapter Seven, below.

not only deeply religious but live in a world which they regard as religious.[9] Their world view is imbued with such a religious disposition that a spiritual condition or state or mode of being is regarded as either forming or influencing the inmost being of nearly every natural object or phenomenon. In other words, almost every natural object or phenomenon is ingrained with a spiritual condition or state or mode of being.

Following the observations of E. A. Ruch and K. C. Anyanwu, I am inclined to conclude that: the Baganda, similar to other Africans, see the sacred dimension in the profane experience of the world; they also see the Absolute Being in a world of which he is not part and parcel.[10] To follow are instances that ought to substantiate this position.

Consider the following examples[11]:

Example 1

Theme: the heavens are infiltrated by spiritual beings and activities[12] -
i. *Ggulu*, the heavens, is the abode of the Absolute Being; hence, the Baganda open their hands in prayer towards the heavens.
ii. Thunder and lightening are produced by the divinity of the sky called *Kiwanuka* as he »beats« the clouds with a big stick.
iii. The clouds originate from the activity of the deity of the River Mayanja as he blows water upward from lakes and rivers.
iv. After spreading that water out into clouds, the deity *Musoke* sends it back to the earth as rain.

---

[9] Cf. Mbiti, J. S. African Religions and Philosophy. Bungay Suffolk, 1985, p. 48. Mbiti's work, here quoted, shall henceforth be referred to as: »Mbiti, J. S. Religions«.

[10] Ruch's and Anyanwu's observations apply mutatis mutandis to the Baganda religious perspective of the universe. Cf. Ruch, E. A./Anyanwu, K. C. African Philosophy. An Introduction to the main Philosophical Trends in Contemporary Africa. Rome, 1981, p. 122

[11] I present these examples in the present tense and in the categorical form. For example, »Ggulu, the heavens, is the abode of the Absolute Being.« In so doing, I am not expressing my personal convictions, but, rather, those of many Baganda, who up until the present day strongly hold such beliefs or positions.

[12] For the following examples I am partly indebted to the works of the authors Kyewalyanga and Mbiti. That is: Kyewalyanga, F. X. op. cit., p. 99; and Mbiti, J. S. Concepts of God in Africa, Southampton, 1970, p. 138. Mbiti's work, here quoted, shall henceforth be referred to as: »Mbiti, J. S. Concepts«.

v. An alternative rendering on the origins of rain considers it to be the spittle of the Absolute Being.
vii. At any rate, rain is a blessing from the heavens for the growth and health of human beings, animals, plants, insects, etc.

Example 2

Theme: Natural objects and living things, e.g., hills, trees, snakes, forests, rocks and places of sacrifice are abodes of spiritual beings [13] –

i. The earth, the ground or soil is inhabited by the earth god called *Kitaka*. He is consulted by gardeners for the fertility of cultivated land and for good harvests.
ii. These hills located in Bulemeezi County in Buganda, Uganda are abodes of the »lion spirits«: Bbowa, Nnambe, Lwanga and Kyangali Hills. They are to be approached with respect and the spirits of these hills have to be appeased with offerings. They are also a safety resort for people fleeing from all sorts of danger.
iii. The following rivers possess spirits which are credited with good or evil powers: Rivers Mayanja, Ssezzibwa and Katonga. An offering to these spirits in the form of coffee berries is hence mandatory before crossing the river.
iv. Many forests are inhabited by nature spirits called »*musambwa* (singular), *misambwa* (plural)«, e.g. the nature spirits Nnabambe and Ntabambe. »*Misambwa*« are consulted by hunters for protection against wild animals and for a successful hunting spree.
v. Besides being abodes of spirits, certain trees are manifestations of those spirits. The nature spirit or »*Musambwa Lubowa*«, for instance, is said to have been a tree at Kalisizo, Buddu County in Buganda.
vi. The python deity »*Sserwanga*« was once a python that had its temple by the River Mujuzi in Buddu County on the shores of Lake Nnalubaale (Victoria). Sserwanga is believed to be a giver of fertility to young couples and is, too, an example of snakes that are manifestations of spirits.
vii. Certain spirits are custodians of places of sacrifice. Before the village Namugongo in Kyaddondo County in Buganda was taken

---

[13] For the following examples I am partly indebted to the work of Roscoe: Roscoe, J. The Baganda. London, 1965, pp. 313–320

over by the Christians, it was »guarded and controlled« by tutelary deities who could even determine when human sacrifices were to be offered there.

Example 3

Theme: Natural and cultural phenomena in the life of the Baganda are associated with spiritual reality.[14]

i. Epidemics, disabilities, major infirmities and diseases are caused by evil spirits. Hence, leprosy, lameness, measles, AIDS, madness, etc are the work of evil spirits or divinities.
ii. The natural colour white expresses a link to supernatural powers. For this reason, one is advised to offer white animal sacrifices, white fouls, white goats, so that the sacred rituals may be accepted by the deities and eventually bear the expected good results. More so, white cocks are kept in homes in order to prevent the lightening deity from sending down this supernatural power to strike that home.
iii. The number nine and its multiples are sacred numbers.
iv. Fire and smoke, too, bear religious symbolism and serve as a link to the spiritual world.
v. Numerous customs, beliefs and taboos express a religious or even a spiritistic outlook towards reality. To comply with the demands of such customs, beliefs and taboos is to show respect to the spirits who are custodians and guardians of the moral and cultural codes of the Baganda society. Such compliance is, however, partly attributed to the fear of being punished by the spirits, say in the case of breaching such codes of conduct.

Besides attempting to provide answers to the question, »Is the world in which the Baganda live spiritistic, or do they perceive »their world« from a fundamentally religious perspective?«, the foregoing lengthy elaboration has highlighted the points given below.

Firstly, vis-à-vis material beings, spiritual beings are ontologically transcendent; in other words, they are considered to be transcending material existence. What is material is consequently regarded as de-

---

[14] For the following examples I am partly indebted to the work of Mbiti: Mbiti, J. S. Concepts, pp. 135–157

pendent upon the spiritual for its activities. Although they are transcendent in status, the spiritual beings find their operative function in the material beings, they are immanent in the material beings, the spiritual is symbolized by the material.[15]

Secondly, the immanence of the spiritual beings in material reality accords special meaning to several natural objects and phenomena. For instance, the validity of given beliefs and customs relies mostly on their being associated with a spiritual being. Without such a normative association, such beliefs or customs would quickly lose their relevance and validity.

Thirdly, the Baganda religious perspective of the world, presented above, cements my argument for their anthropocentric view of the universe. How? The spiritual beings, by virtue of their being immanent in material reality, count in either the category of security, which incorporates beings that are serviceable, valuable, beneficial, etc. to the human being, or in the category of precariousness, which embodies beings that are hazardous, harmful, etc. to the human being.

A »Stratificational« World view / The Three Worlds

The fact that the Baganda Weltanschauung is on the one hand anthropocentric, and on the other hand religious or spiritistic, suggests a division or an arrangement of beings into a series of graded statuses. To put it in other words, there is in the universe a state of being stratified; hence the discussion about a stratificational world view.

Several reasons compel me to think that: according to Baganda Ntu'ology, there are three types of »worlds«: the supra-spiritual world, the spiritual world and the physical world. The first two »worlds« are invisible, while the last one is visible.

The supra-spiritual world consists of »Katonda«. His name means »creator«. While he himself has neither beginning nor end,[16] he is the creator of everything; he is the Absolute Being of the Baganda. Michael

---

[15] Like Anyanwu and Ruch write about other Africans, I, too, am of the opinion that among the Baganda, the sacred is not merely symbolized by the profane. Rather, the sacred permeates the profane, lives and moves in it. Seen concretely, however, it is the profane which is the symbol that renders the sacred visible. See Ruch, E. A./Anyanwu, K. C. op. cit., p. 123

[16] On this matter, see Kyewalyanga, F. X. op. cit., p. 99

Nsimbi supports this note on Katonda's necessity and eternity when he holds that the God of the Baganda has no father nor mother nor children; his only function is to create.[17] *Katonda* is additionally the »father of the gods«; the gods are among his creatures.[18] What the the Baganda present as their knowledge of *Katonda* is on the one hand sufficient stuff to offer us a fair idea about him. On the other hand, however, it is too little material to exhaust his nature and function.

Moreover, *Katonda* counts in the category of security, which incorporates beings that are serviceable, valuable, beneficial, etc. to the human being. All in all, Katonda is a spiritual being; but, among the spiritual beings, he is a supra-spiritual being.

The spiritual world covers the whole range of spiritual beings excluding *Katonda*. Baganda Ntu'ology classifies these spiritual beings thus:

i. The divinities, deities or gods; they are named »*balubaale* (plural) or *lubaale* (singular)«, and are a class higher than the rest of the spiritual beings;

ii. a) The ordinary spirits or ghosts are called »*mizimu* (plural) or *muzimu* (singular)«;

ii. b) The fetishes also known as »*mayembe* (plural) or *jjembe* (singular)«; and

iii. c) The nature spirits are named »*misambwa* (plural) or *musambwa* (singular)«.[19]

The physical world envelops human beings and what I earlier on termed physical beings of the Kintu category or the physical *bintu*. The latter group encompasses all sorts of animals, plants, in-animates, etc. It is held that the human being rules over all the beings in the physical world. With the aid of a diagram (Diagram 1), I intend to demonstrate the Baganda »stratificational« world-outlook.

---

[17] Consider Nsimbi, M. B. op.cit., p. 40
[18] Ibidem, p. 139.
[19] Since these three minor categories of spiritual beings stem from the spiritual element of the human being, we shall treat the themes »*mizimu, mayembe and misambwa*« in more details in Chapters 5 and 10 below.

Aspect two Baganda Ntu'ology Categorization

Diagram 1 The Pyramidal Strata of Being

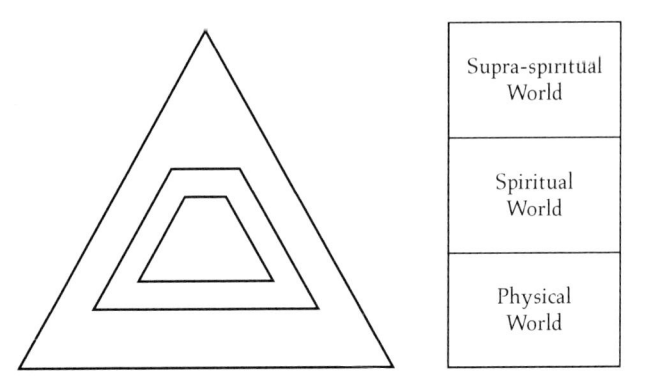

	Supra-spiritual World
	Spiritual World
	Physical World

This diagram as such and its title in particular exhibit my idea of the Baganda stratificational world view by means of two outstanding features. In the first instance, there is the association with a pyramid; and, in the second instance, the diagram bears a tripartite form.

By according this diagram a pyramidal form, I highlight the significant feature of any pyramid, i. e. »the narrowing gradually towards an apex«. This feature brings to light the point that, the being of beings, in Baganda Ntu'ology, varies qualitatively and quantitatively; hence the title, »the pyramidal strata of being.« The broad supporting base of the pyramid (the physical world) presupposes, on the one hand, a larger number of beings (which can be directly perceived by the human being) than the middle part or the apex of the same pyramid. On the other hand, the narrower the pyramid becomes, the higher the quality of being.

Furthermore, the tripartite form borne by the diagram indicates two things: firstly, it denotes the Baganda Ntu'ological view point of the »three worlds«: the supra-spiritual, the spiritual and the physical worlds. Secondly, it sketches the immanence of spiritual beings in material reality. That is, Katonda, the Absolute Being is not only immanent in the spiritual world of the spiritual »*bintu*«, but also in the physical world. Accordingly, the apex of the pyramid, which represents his supra-spiritual world, extends downwards to encompass the two inner quadrangles. More so, the spiritual »*bintu*« are immanent in the physical world. Hence, the middle part of the pyramid, representing the spiritual world, extends downwards to envelop the innermost quadrangle.

The antecedent section has presented the Absolute Being as a creator; his name is *Katonda*, the creator. Derived from the Luganda verb »*kutonda*«, i.e. to create or to bring into existence, the substantive »*Katonda*« refers to that which, or the one who creates the universe.[20]

The Baganda confess the continuous sustenance and providence of God towards that what he created, the universe. He is immanent in all forces that could be counted in the category of security, which incorporates beings that are serviceable, valuable, beneficial, etc. to the human being. Hence his other name, »*Ssewannaku*,« i.e., the ever-present. *Katonda* is immanent and the Baganda are conscious of this. This is the type of consciousness that Anyanwu and Ruch term a quasi empirical, intuitive awareness of the sacred.[21]

Viewed against the background of the above given notes on *Katonda*, the universe is, in the mind of the Baganda, dependent upon and conditioned by *Katonda*. It depends on *Katonda*, as the necessary being, the creator of all reality and values, of the spiritual and physical worlds, of the universe and all laws, customs, taboos, regulations, institutions, etc. The world, according to the Baganda, is therefore a contingent world.

A Dynamic Universe

Besides maintaining that the world as conceived by the Baganda is a contingent world, it has so far been argued that the Baganda eltanschauung consists of a world-view that is anthropocentric, religiospiritistic and »stratificational.« To be added to these perspectives is the Baganda-view of the world as a dynamic universe. Considered from this angle, the world or the universe is permeated by a certain dynamism which is at times described as a force, and which manifests itself in several distinct ways. I shall henceforth refer to this dynamism in the universe as »*amaanyi*«.[22]

---

[20] Katonda is also named »*Namugereka*« (planner) and »*Kagingo*« (chief designer) of all things, of the whole universe. For further information on this matter, see, especially, Kyewalyanga, F. X. op. cit., p. 99
[21] Cf. Ruch, E. A./Anyanwu, K. C. op. cit., p. 123
[22] The Luganda word *amaanyi* designates strength, force, dynamism, power.

»Amaanyi«, the All Reality Permeating Dynamism

Amaanyi is a quality or expression of being. It is not an independent force existing independent of the beings in the universe. *Amaanyi* designates a principle of activity in beings. It expresses itself in the form of a dynamism, power, force that permeates and, too, emanates from reality. The inanimate entities in the Kintu category, the inanimate physical *bintu*, too, are permeated with *amaanyi,* and they, so to speak, radiate it outwards. In the »Baganda world«, matter is not inert but rather active, since it is permeated with *amaanyi*. In the Baganda sense of the word, »to be« is »to be with *amaanyi*.«

The Baganda hold the belief that *Katonda*, as the primogenitor of the spiritual beings and the creator of the whole universe, is the source and ultimate guide of *amaanyi*.

Katonda, it is maintained, deals out *amaanyi* to the spiritual beings of the Kintu category or the spiritual *bintu*. It is through the spiritual *bintu*, that *Katonda* dispenses *amaanyi* to the physical beings. It is no wonder, then, that certain physical beings which are said to be endowed with *amaanyi* in a special way, are always associated with a certain spiritual being, say, a nature spirit. Such a physical being is, in this regard, held to be the abode of that nature spirit.

Notwithstanding the belief that all existents are media of the all-reality-permeating-dynamism, *amaanyi* is, nonetheless, held by the Baganda as manifesting itself to human beings outstandingly in spectacular natural objects, and in persons of rank, note or distinction. In this connection, physical beings like boulders, hills, trees of gigantic size or height, principal rivers, etc are considered to display *amaanyi* in a special manner. Similarly, personages like *Kabaka*, the king, and the elders manifest *amaanyi* in a peculiar way.[23]

The different modes of the manifestation of *amaanyi* may be qualified as »attractional,« horrid or neutral. This qualification is basically influenced by the Baganda's anthropocentric view of the world.[24] That

---

[23] No wonder, the Baganda maintain that personages like the king and elders manifest *amaanyi* in a peculiar way. *Kabaka*, the king, is after all a spiritual leader uniting the physical world of the human beings with the spiritual world of the spirits. The elders, in their turn, are held to be nearest to the eldest of the old, i.e. to *Katonda*.

[24] Compare this classification with the categorization, presented under Section 5.1.1, above, which included: the category of security, the category of precariousness, and, the category of neutrality.

is, even the nature or mode of manifestation of *amaanyi* is classified depending upon the value and significance of the particular mode of that manifestation to the human being.

Consequently, a single mode of manifestation of *amaanyi* is:
i. »Attractional,« if it is regarded to be helpful, serviceable, valuable, beneficial, etc. to the human being; or
ii. Horrid, if it is considered as frightful, hazardous, harmful, etc. to the human being; or
iii. Neutral, if is deemed to be indifferently disposed to the human being.

A simple instance that exhibits an »attractional« mode of the manifestation of *amaanyi*, is the »Baganda's flocking willingly to the palace of *Kabaka*«. Such visits to their king are not the result of an act, process or power of coercion. Rather, people feel attracted to their spiritual leader, the king, who, according to their strong belief, unites the physical world of the human beings with the spiritual world of the spirits. *Kabaka*, the king, is hence regarded as possessing *amaanyi* in an »attractional« manner.

There are, however, examples of beings which possess *amaanyi* in a way that is frightful or hazardous or harmful, etc to the human being. Consider boulders, hills, thickets which have to be approached only with due prudence and circumspection. One has, so to speak, to be so careful in approaching such places as to consider all circumstances and possible consequences of whatever one says and/or does there. Such places are hence regarded to be possessing *amaanyi* in a horrid manner.

There are, too, beings, for instance tiny insects, harmless animals, etc., which are in most cases are too weak to be dangerous to the human being or his/her environment. Such beings are deemed to be indifferently disposed to the human being. They are considered, hence, to possess *amaanyi* in a neutral manner.

It has been noted above, that for the Baganda »to be« is »to be with *amaanyi*«. That is, *amaanyi* unites thoroughly with each and every existent, *amaanyi* works indistinguishably into each and every existent. Consequently, all existents are in their innermost nature media of *amaanyi*. Conceived from this point of view of all existents being media of *amaanyi*, existence may be described as the mutual or reciprocal action or influence prevailing between the various media of *amaanyi*.

Aspect two   Baganda Ntu'ology Categorization

Consequently, through their being media of *amaanyi*, all existents are ontologically related to each other both at the accidental, superficial level of their interactions, as well as at the deeper level of their being. Baganda Ntu'ology thus, accommodates no isolated mode of being. To have *amaanyi* is »to be in relation to« something.

A last but one note about this all-reality-permeating-dynamism concerns the Baganda's love for what I name the »profound searching for causes.« There prevails among these people a peculiar type of dissatisfaction with regarding physical causality as a sufficient explanation of the phenomena occurring in, and influencing the life and environment of the human being. For instance, falling sick may not be simply accepted as the result of being infected with, say, a certain virus. Rather, there must be alternative or additional explanations to this »being infected with a virus.«

It appears to me, that the »alternative or additional explanations« which the Baganda sigh for – when geared by their love for profound searching for causes –, lie in the mutual or reciprocal action or influence prevailing between the various media of *amaanyi*. Since some of the media of *amaanyi* are spiritual beings, the »alternative or additional explanations« lie beyond the material, physical, visible causes. They lie in the spiritual world and are consequently accessible to only those human beings endowed with special powers, e. g. medicine-men.

I shall let this rather lengthy elaboration on amaanyi die at the following point of observation: *amaanyi* is that type of dynamism which remains or operates, to a very large extent, within a domain of reality that is directly or indirectly accessible to the human being. That which the Baganda may describe as a power, a force, or that which I have so far termed the all-reality-permeating-dynamism is, to my contention, the immanence of the spiritual beings in material reality. We noted above, that *Katonda*, the Absolute Being is not only immanent in the spiritual world of the spiritual »*bintu*«, but also in the physical world; and, that the spiritual »*bintu*« are immanent in the physical world.

It is this *amaanyi*, this »immanence of the spiritual in the material« which confers sacredness to the universe. For the Baganda, the universe is not only contingent. It is as well sacred, since *Katonda* and the spiritual beings that are inferior to him manifest their being and presence in the universe through varied or various media of *amaanyi*. Accordingly, those physical objects or persons that manifest *amaanyi* in a peculiar way are not only considered as sharers in the being of spiritual entities, they are also venerated by the Baganda.[25]

Furthermore, *amaanyi* confers unity to the universe. Accordingly, what I previously referred to as »the three worlds« are realms of the universe that are, for the Baganda, inseparably united. The diagram presented in that section exhibits that the three worlds are so inextricably interwoven that one hardly attempts to determine exactly the borders between them.

---

[25] According to Lugira, these objects are venerated, since they are manifestations of the sacred which people honour, placate and petition in order to assure some security and survival against difficult odds. See Lugira, A. M. op. cit., p. 116

Aspect three
Muntu-centrism in Baganda Ntu'ology

With a series of arguments, it has been demonstrated in the fore-going chapter that the Baganda hold the human being to be the centre of the universe. The most outstanding instance so far noted is their tendency to interpret the world in terms of human experience and values, i.e. the world outlook which I have termed an anthropocentric *Weltanschauung*.

There are as well other instances which substantiate what I shall name »Muntu-centrism« in Baganda Ntu'ology. These »other instances« are our concern in the coming six chapters, Chapters 5 to 10. Taken together, these chapters highlight further the phenomenon of concentrating awareness and understanding of reality and values about the human being, a phenomenon that I have named »Muntu-centrism.«

Similar to the case of the three special terms used in the chapters of Aspect Two, the word »integralistic« shall be used in chapters of Aspect Three instead of the more familiar adjective »integral« to highlight particular Baganda Ntu'ological issues.

Chapter five
Muntu'ology

»*Muntu'ology*« is a sub-division of Baganda Ntu'ology. By »*muntu'ology*«, I allude to wisdom that is the basic principle for a classification of reality and values according to the *Muntu* category of being. Beyond adequately developing the ideas presented in the fourth chapter about the category of existents with human intelligence or the *Muntu* category, this chapter establishes the foundation upon which I shall depend, in the next chapters, to analyse and/or interpret the inter-relationship between the entities in this NTU category and the rest of reality and values.

Muntu: The Human Being

Muntu, the singular form of *Bantu*, means »human being« or »human person.« But, where does *muntu* come from? The Baganda appear not to speculate much about the origins of *muntu*. It is hence not surprising to note that even the most popular account about the origin of *muntu* does not mention specifically and exactly where the man named Kintu came from.[1]

However, like we stated in the antecedent chapter, *muntu*, it is believed by the Baganda, was created by *Katonda*.[2] *Muntu* is part and parcel of the contingent world which *Katonda* created and still sustains.

Regarding the basic constitution of the human being, Baganda Ntu'ology tends to a course of analysis which, since it comprehends or

---

[1] Cf. Roscoe J., op. cit., p. 461.
In one of his famous books, E. K. N. Kawere collects a number of fables, myths, etc that, nevertheless, provide scanty information about issues related to the origin of the human being; for instance, regarding the origin of death, the origin certain characteristic actions of given animals, etc. See Kawere, E. K. N., Bukadde Magezi. Nairobi, 1968.
[2] Regarding the activity of the creator, *Katonda*, consider sub-section 5.1.4, above.

unites more than two features that make up the unity called *muntu*, is different from the dichotomous descriptions of Western Philosophy[3]. The subsequent sections substantiate my argument that: against the descriptive background of that manifold course of analysis in Baganda Ntu'ology, *muntu* is not conceived by the Baganda as a duality, but, rather as a unity.

»Omubiri«: Beyond the Human Body

A significant feature of *muntu* is *omubiri*. The English word that is closest in meaning to *omubiri* is the »body«[4]. Beyond being simply the physical substance, the material part or nature of the human being, *omubiri* expresses the dimension of life in the human being. *Omubiri* is the immediate subject of good or bad health. This word is thus intimately associated with the living human being. Consequently, the dead physical substance, the dead material part or nature of the human being is not called *omubiri*, it is, rather, known as *omulambo or enjole;* that is, »a corpse«.[5]

A prominent characteristic of *omubiri* is *omukka*. *Omukka*, which usually means a »gas«, »smoke«, or »air inhaled and exhaled in breathing«, does not only further signify the faculty of breathing, but is the life sustaining thread. Dying naturally or being killed is therefore often described in terms of the loss of this feature of *omubiri*, i. e., the deprivation of this sign of being alive. On this matter, consider the following examples:

i. Example 1: »*Okumiza omuntu omukka omusu*«, literally means, »to coerce someone to breathe in hot air.« The actual meaning is: to murder someone.
ii. Example 2: »*Okussa omukka omuvannyuma*«, literally means, »to take the last breath.« The direct meaning is: to die.

---

[3] Specific reference is made hereby to the division of the human being into body or matter and soul or mind.
[4] I find it difficult to translate this word or concept into English, since the term *omubiri* bears a varied range of meanings. It may serve to signify the body, the skin, the physical stature of an individual, etc.
[5] *Omulambo* refers to the dead body of a person who is not of royal descent, while *enjole* implies the non-living body of a king.

Omukka is hence both a significant »life supply line« for *omubiri*, as well as a »borderline« between *omubiri* and *omulambo*. That is, the moment *omukka* is interrupted, *omubiri* becomes *omulambo*, since from this moment onwards, »*omubiri*« no longer expresses the dimension of life in the human being. *Omukka* is hence that prominent characteristic of *omubiri* that abets the dimension of life in the human being.

Muntu'ology tends towards seeking correspondence in meaning between given human organic processes or phenomena or human anatomical parts, and the basic socio-psychological disposition of the human being, of *muntu*. The foregoing elaboration on *omukka* and the subsequent observations regarding *omutima* (the heart), *emmeeme* (the tip of the sternum) and *omusaayi* (the blood) are good examples on that matter.

Omutima, generally considered, means the »heart«, the pump force or organ which maintains the circulation of blood in vertebrate animals. Hereby it refers specifically to the human physical heart. The following instances illustrate the Baganda's search for correspondence in meaning between this human anatomical organ and given basic socio-psychological dispositions of the human being.

i. <u>Instance 1 –</u>
a) The day-to-day expression: »*Omuntu ow'omutima omulungi.*«
b) Its literal meaning: »A person with a good heart.«
c) Its strict meaning: »A good-willed person.«

ii. <u>Instance 2 –</u>
a) The day-to-day expression: »*Omutima gwambuuseemu.*«
b) Its literal meaning: »My heart sprung free from me.«
c) Its strict meaning: »I was terribly frightened.«

iii. <u>Instance 3 –</u>
a) The day-to-day expression: »*Omuntu eyafa omutima.*«
b) Its literal meaning: »A person with a dead heart.«
c) Its strict meaning: »A person having a dead conscience.«

Omutima, seen from the perspective of the above stated, has this derived meaning: it is the seat of the psychological faculties, the depth of the personality of the human being, of *muntu*. *Omutima* is therefore a primary source, a principle of human nature, a principle that underlyies the socio-psychological and moral disposition of the human being, of *muntu*.

Furthermore, the tip of the compound ventral bone connecting the ribs, i.e. *emmeeme*, too, has a »meta-physical« meaning in Muntu'ology. The subsequent instances may highlight this theory.

i. <u>Instance 1 -</u>
a) The saying: »*Emmeeme gy'esula n'ebigere gyebikeera.*«
b) Its literal meaning: »The place at which the tip of the sternum spends the night, becomes the first destination of the feet on the following day.«
c) Its strict meaning: »Where one's heart's desire lies, there is the base of one's emotional activity.«

ii. <u>Instance 2 -</u>
a) The day-to-day expression: »*Omuntu eyagwa emmeeme.*«
b) Its literal meaning: »A person whose tip of the sternum dropped low or down.«
c) Its strict meaning: »A person who has lost appetite.«

iii. <u>Instance 3 -</u>
a) The saying: »*Emmeeme eteebuuza, efubutula eggambo.*«
b) Its literal meaning: »The tip of the sternum which does not consult or ask for advise, utters a foolish word.«
c) Its strict meaning: »An emotional person is liable to use slang or vulgar abuse.«

Emmeeme, considered from the view point of the above stated, has this derived meaning: it is the seat of the emotional functions or traits of the human being, of *muntu*. In contrast to *omutima*, *emmeeme* is a minor source or principle of human nature, a principle that underlies several emotions and appetites of the human being, of *muntu*.

Omusaayi is yet another prominent feature of the human being, a dimension of the human being which acquires its name as a result of the Baganda's search for correspondence in meaning between a certain human anatomical organ or a physiological process and given basic socio-psychological dispositions of the human being. Accordingly, *omusaayi*, which literally means »blood«, has as well a »meta-physical« meaning: it signifies the link between the individual and his/her extended family. *Omusaayi*, in my phraseology, is that what one inherits from one's father and qualifies one to be a member of the extended family or clan. Hence, *omusaayi* is the principle of human nature underlying the social interactions of the human being, of *muntu*.

»Omuzimu«: Is it the Human Soul?

The Baganda employ the same term for the non-material dimension of the living human being, as well as for the spiritual beings of the Kintu category, the spiritual *bintu* as I named them. The common term is, »*omuzimu*«. Consequently, *omuzimu* means both the spiritual element of the living human being and the ordinary spirits or ghosts. It follows, then, that while every living human being, every *muntu* must have *omuzimu*, and not every *muzimu* is *muntu*.

Elaborating on the media of *amaanyi*, the all-reality-permeating-dynamism, we observed that, in accordance with the mind of the Baganda, Katonda dispenses *amaanyi* to the physical beings through the spiritual beings. I am inclined to think that it is by virtue of *omuzimu* that *amaanyi* can be dealt out to the human being, to the *muntu*.

Omuzimu is, hence, a very significant element in the transmission of *amaanyi*. Consider, for instance, the following chain of the transmission of *amaanyi*. Being its ultimate source and guide, Katonda deals out *amaanyi* to the spiritual beings of the Kintu category or the spiritual *bintu*. It is through the spiritual *bintu* that Katonda dispenses *amaanyi* to the human being, to the *muntu*. It is by means of *omuzimu* that Katonda finally deals out *amaanyi* to the *muntu*. I therefore hold that, for the human being, *omuzimu* is the immediate form of the manifestation of the »immanence of the spiritual in the material.« It is *muntu*'s personal medium of *amaanyi*.

Consequently, during his/her life, the human being, the *muntu* attains what I may call a »partial assimilation into the spiritual world« by virtue of his/her *muzimu*. Moreso, *omuzimu*, as that what survives the human being, is the means towards a full assimilation into the spiritual world of the ancestors.

The visible or most overt manifestation of *omuzimu* is, so the Baganda, the shadow cast by the body of the *muntu*. *Ekisikirize* is the Luganda word for that shadow. In Muntu'ology, the shadow is so vital an element of *muntu*'s being, that his/her existence in the physical world is said to continue only so long as he/she has a shadow. *Ekisikirize* is accorded such remarkable relevance, because it is considered to be an externalization and/or an extension of the individual's *muzimu*.

An »Integralistic« Conception of Muntu

Basing myself on the antecedent illustration regarding the human being, the *muntu*, I may rightly conclude that, according to Muntu'ology, a purely dualistic conception of the human being has to be rejected as an over-simplification of this significant issue. That is, while the Baganda concur with the view that the nature of *muntu* comprises both somatic and spiritual dimensions, their mind tends towards what I may term an *integralistic conception* of the human being.

What I term an integralistic conception of the *muntu* is, firstly, the general idea of the human being which admits the presence of both somatic and spiritual dimensions in the nature of the human being. It is, secondly, the theoretical summary or product of the Baganda's ideas and beliefs regarding the *muntu*, a summary or product that presents the human being as a unity composed of several integral parts.

Chapter six
Muntu knows other »Ntu«

That *muntu* is a self-aware individual who knows other »NTU«[1] – to include the other human beings –, is yet another instance which substantiates further my views on the phenomenon of concentrating awareness and understanding of reality and values about the human being, a phenomenon that I have named »Muntu-centrism.«

The condensed sentence, »Muntu knows other ›NTU‹«, is a statement regarding the concept of knowledge, specifically, knowledge in Baganda Ntu'ology. But, what is knowledge in Baganda Ntu'ology?

Muntu Knows

The Luganda verb that expresses the act of knowing is »*okumanya*«. The name derived from this verb, the noun that ought to be given to the act or action of knowing, is *obumanyirivu*. *Obumanyirivu*, however, refers to what common language terms practical knowledge. *Obumanyirivu* is skill or practice derived from the experience of personally or directly participating in, encountering, undergoing, or living through an event or events.

One observes from the above given description that the noun *obumanyirivu* lays more accent on the effect or products of knowledge than on the nature and sources of this problem.

Amagezi is yet another Luganda term that expresses the act or action of knowing. It would appear that this word *amagezi* tells more about knowledge than *obumanyirivu*.

---

[1] We may want to widen our learning about this characteristic of knowledge, i.e. the human being, in general, being a »self-aware individual« and »that for which there are objects to be known«, by considering: Mutaawe Kasozi, F. The Self and Social Reality in a Philosophical Anthropology, Frankfurt am Main, 1998, pp. 135–139.

Aspect three   Muntu-centrism in Baganda Ntu'ology

At first analysis, the Luganda word *amagezi* might seem to refer to a unit of experience that is in one way or another separate from knowledge, since it, *amugezi*, simply means a wise attitude, a wise course of action or simply »wisdom«. However, by analysing a variety of contextual meanings of *amagezi*, we learn more about knowledge in Baganda Ntu'ology, both about knowledge as *muntu's* consciousness of himself/herself and of the other NTU around him/her, and about the genesis and utility of this awareness to *muntu*.

Amagezi refers, in the first place, to *muntu's* intellectual understanding of, and/or intellectual acquaintance with something. This meaning is implied in common sayings like: »*Abuulira omugezi takoowa.*«[2] In this context, *amagezi* is that what inevitably follows antecedents like, fast comprehension, the ability to make the right inference, a sharp memory, etc. In other words, an antecedent like fast comprehension counts in one way or another as the cause or agent of *amagezi*.

Regarded as *muntu's* intellectual understanding of, and/or intellectual acquaintance with something, *amagezi* is said to be greatly influenced by one's heredity. It is hence further described as *amagezi amazaale*.[3]

In some instances, amagezi expresses the kind of muntu's self-consciousness and his/her awareness of the other NTU around him/her which follow naturally the actual, personal or indirect experience of muntu's intellectual understanding of, and/or intellectual acquaintance with something. It is the type of consciousness acquired due muntu's ability to retain mental images from, or memory of a good number of experiences.

Amagezi, in this context, is that reality consciousness borne out of actual experience(s). It is therefore that extensive knowledge possessed in a special manner by the elders and the elderly of a family or clan. It is

---

[2] The saying literally means: one who explains things to a wise or intelligent person does not get tired (of talking). That is, the listener does not weary the narrator with ennui or tedium, since the former's intellectual understanding of what is being narrated is high.

[3] *Amagezi amazaale*, literally means »innate wisdom«. This expression does not, however, mean that knowledge is innate or inborn. Rather, it refers to the potential for the intellectual understanding of, and/or intellectual acquaintance with reality, i.e., that potential which is part of the sum of the qualities and potentialities genetically derived from one's ancestors. Consider, for instance, the common expression, »*amagezi gano (amazaale) g'ebukojja.*« That means, (the child has) intellectual potential genetically derived from (its) matrilineal ancestors.

also termed »the wisdom of the elders.«[4] Those who possess *amagezi* of this kind, i.e., by virtue of their status and/or age, are regarded, among the Baganda, as consultants or even judges. Their long experience in regard to the intellectual understanding of, and/or intellectual acquaintance with reality equips them with the ability to give advice[5], and thus, too, with the ability to adjudicate in certain situations.

Any theoretical method designed for making or doing something or attaining an end may be termed *amagezi*. It is in this vein that one refers to »designing a plan or plot« as *okusala amagezi*. The experience upon which one depends to exploit, to manipulate the world around one may be referred to as *amagezi*. The knowledge underlying a method or plan that one designs to save oneself from an impeding danger or to live through a dangerous situation is also *amagezi*. In this sense, *amagezi* is that intellectual or mental theory that underlies a plan, design, plot, scheme, project, etc.

Close to the foregoing category of *amagezi* is the intellectual or mental theory that underlies one's tactfulness for the sake of achieving either good, useful purposes, or bad, mischievous ends. Referring to tactfulness for mischievous ends, the Baganda employ, for example, the following expressions: *okusala amagezi aga Wakayima* or *okusala amagezi ag'enkolwa*.[6]

From a technical point of view, *amagezi* is that intellectual or mental theory which underlies a practical skill; for instance, the skill of producing bark-cloth, clay pots, etc.

An individual's constant awareness of the fact that he/she ought to live in harmony with fellow human beings qualifies that kind of consciousness as *amagezi*. Accordingly, etiquette, courtesy, sociability are

---

[4] Consider the saying: »*Obukadde magezi, takubuulira kyamukaddiya.*« I take the academic liberty to translate it, thus: Although old age is wisdom, an elderly person is not obliged to recite the details of his/her life-story. The equation, »old age equals wisdom« is of striking importance here.

[5] The Luganda expression for »to give advice« is: »*okuwa amagezi*«; which literally means »to give wisdom or knowledge«. The act of giving advice is therefore a situation of transmitting knowledge, on the one hand, and an act of acquiring knowledge, on the other hand.

[6] These expressions mean: »to play the tricks of a hare« and »to play the tricks of a mongoose«, respectively. Baganda oral tradition presents the hare and the mongoose as very clever animals. When, for instance, the mongoose is struck, it lies down and plays dead in order to avoid a second or harder beating.

key elements of *amagezi*. »Respecting elders« is, for instance, at times expressed in words that mean »knowing the elders«; i.e., *okumanya abakulu*. »Being sociable« is similarly referred to as »knowing people«; i.e. *okumanya abantu*.

In this connection, too, »behaving well« is often times expressed in words that mean »having knowledge or wisdom«; i.e. *okuba n'amagezi*. Behaving in a manner opposite to what is expected or accepted is demonstrating the lack of the awareness of the fact that one ought to live in harmony with fellow human beings, the lack of *amagezi*.[7]

The above-given observations present knowledge, in Baganda Ntu'ology, as the consciousness borne out of cognition-related experiences or processes which may be mental or intellectual, or actual or practical. This consciousness has both personal and social dimensions. The latter dimension does not only embrace the awareness of social reality around the individual *muntu*, but also directs and guides his/her social interactions with the others.

Muntu Acquires Knowledge

A very relevant question here is: does Baganda Ntu'ology »believe« that some concepts or ideas are independent of experience and that some truth is known by reason alone, or does it »believe« that all concepts or ideas rise from experience and that truth must be established

---

[7] The equation »ethical/moral behaviour equals knowledge/wisdom« may help us to appreciate a certain manner of reprimanding an individual who misbehaves. The respective individual is often times exposed to a mode of satirical wit that presents him/her as »having little knowledge or wisdom«. Such sarcasm often entails a mode of ironic, caustic or even bitter language by means of which that individual is made to appear as »having less knowledge or wisdom« than, for instance, a domestic fowl. Consider the common abusive expression: »*Enkoko ekusinza amagezi*«; that is, »the domestic fowl is wiser than you are.«

Although the, so to speak, moral/ethical behaviour teacher of that individual does not actually imply that the latter »has less knowledge or wisdom« than a domestic fowl, the former accentuates thereby the point that »behaving well« is »having knowledge or wisdom«.

The moral/ethical behaviour teacher also emphasises, in an sarcastic way, that in *doing what is expected* of it, the domestic fowl, so to say, »has knowledge or wisdom«, while the human being who *does what is not morally or ethically expected* of him/her, comparatively said, »has less knowledge or wisdom« than the domestic fowl in question.

by reference to experience alone? Baganda Ntu'ology »answers« this question in multiple ways.

Personal, immediate experience is considered by the Baganda to be the source of very reliable truths. The physical world as a key object of human knowledge, and the senses as »the media« of perception play very essential roles in that experience. It is, for instance, demanded by the Baganda cultural law court judges that a person whose testimony is to be regarded as true, must demonstrate that he/she had direct sense contact with the objective physical world in the process of his/her knowing what he/she claims to be true.[8] That person's statements are said to hold true information or knowledge, if they are related to the historical state of affairs by means of demonstrative conventions, say, seeing, hearing, touching, etc.

In most cases this personal, immediate experience, and, consequently the knowledge accruing there from, are acquired by means of the senses. The role of the senses in the acquisition of knowledge is regarded to be very essential, as the following analysis demonstrates. The saying, »*ekiri mu ttu kimanyibwa nnyinikyo*«[9] permits us to drawn an analogy between the world or the physical objects around a given individual and a sealed parcel. The contents of such a parcel may get exposed by means of a certain instrument that one employs for that purpose. Likewise, the physical world around us becomes known to us as it gets exposed by means of the senses.

The essential role of the senses in the acquisition of knowledge is further demonstrated by what I shall term the »*katulabe syndrome*« prevailing among the Baganda. »*Katulabe*« means »let us see«. In the search for certitude, the Baganda often times wish to physically touch and see the object in question. The derived meaning of »*katulabe*« is, therefore: »let us touch and see the object.« The *katulabe syndrome* is also expressed in the popular saying: »*Amaaso g'Omuganda gali mu*

---

[8] For further information on this matter, see Mutaawe Kasozi, F. The Ganda Traditional Law Court Processes and Syllogistic Inference, (Unpublished Essay). Katigondo/Masaka, February 21, 1983; especially, Chapter 3, pp. 17–21.

[9] The saying literally means: the contents of a sealed parcel are known (almost exclusively) by its owner. It is a point worthy noting that the owner referred to here is that person who, while he/she did not pack and seal the parcel, has now the right to disclose the contents, and consequently, has the privilege of knowing the contents. Particular reference is made to the owner who, so to speak, had no fore-knowledge about the contents of the parcel.

ngalo«. It literally means, »the eyes of a Muganda are in his/her hands.« What underlies this *katulabe syndrome* is not only the search for certitude or external evidence, but also the significant role of the senses in establishing knowledge. In order that the particular corporeal datum become objective and real, it ought to be perceptible to several senses.

By noting the contrast between the next two proverbs, one observes that although the role of the senses in the acquisition of knowledge is regarded to be very essential, the senses here in question must be in a sound bodily condition. The proverbs are: »*Kumala biseera nga abuulira kiggala«*; and »*Abuulira omugezi takoowa«*. The former literally means: it is wastage of precious time to talk to a deaf person; and the latter: one who narrates things to an intelligent person need not tire himself out talking. That is, while in the first case deafness is a hindrance to acquiring knowledge, there is, in the second case, the very high degree of attention to what is being narrated which is facilitated by listener's superb intellectual power to know.

It is not sufficient that one possesses the necessary senses. The acquisition of knowledge also presupposes a good level of co-ordination between the action of the senses and the intellectual power to know. This good level of co-ordination could, on the one hand, be established by simple means, say, by paying attention to what is being said. On the other hand, however, it could be impaired by physical disability, or simply, by stubbornness. On this matter, consider these proverbs: »*Abuulira alowooza, asirika akira«*; that is, it is better to keep quiet than talk to an absent-minded person. »*Enkuba tejjuza bumoome«*; that means literally, »rain does not fill the openings of an ant hill.« The latter set of proverbs applies to a person who, due physical disability, is slow at understanding, or to one who, out of stubbornness, fails to grasp the truth of the matter.

Besides demonstrating the essential role the senses play in the acquisition of knowledge, the previous sub-section builds an argument for the point that knowledge is often times procured through an agent. The process of giving testimony is a good example of acquiring knowledge through an intermediary. Among the Baganda, verbal testimony is not limited to a solemn declaration which is usually made orally by a witness as an answer to interrogation by a lawyer or an authorized public official. Rather, it is, too, any authentication of a fact made orally by a responsible person.

Consider, for instance, the message of this proverb: »*Gyebanzaliira mmanyiyo; ng'alina nnyina eyamubuulira.*« That is, having been duly informed by one's mother about one's exact place of birth, one may rightly claim to know that place. This means further that, in spite of having once been a baby or a little child, one may later acquire knowledge about one's childhood through the spoken word of, say, the mother.

Viewed from a personal point of view, the class of the elders includes: one's parents, local government chiefs, family and clan leaders and religious leaders. These personalities play a key role in the process of transmitting or acquiring knowledge. In most cases, the Baganda accept the verbal testimony of an elder not barely as unquestionable truth, but also as true and certain knowledge.

The elders have *amagezi,* that reality consciousness which is borne out of multiple actual experience(s). Due to their age or experience or privileged status, the elders possess extensive knowledge about many aspects of life, about tribal customs and laws, religious ceremonies and rites, etc. They have the duty of supplementing and guiding the personal experience of the young(er) generation by, to put it categorically, passing on knowledge to them.

The mediation of knowledge by verbal testimony is, for the Baganda, not exclusively interpersonal or a matter between human beings only. Rather, the spiritual beings, too, are believed to play a very significant role in this regard.[10] Since the spiritual beings are, in Baganda Ntu'ology too, the living-dead,[11] they are believed to continue caring for the living. One of the forms of that care is the passing on information, at times vital information about things one might otherwise not have known. The media employed by spiritual beings in transmitting knowledge may be human beings, say the diviners and dream interpreters, and/or phenomena, like special dreams.

A message from a spiritual being is ranked higher than even the verbal testimony of an elder. It is hence regarded not only as unquestionable truth of the first order, but also as significantly true and cer-

---

[10] The view that the spiritual beings play a significant role in the mediation of knowledge entails overtones of what we observed, in the fourth chapter, about the Baganda's religious or spiritistic perspective of reality, or about their idea of an all-reality-permeating-dynamism.

[11] On the notion of the living-dead, see also Mbiti, J. S. Religions, p. 25

Aspect three Muntu-centrism in Baganda Ntu'ology

tain knowledge. Oral tradition has it that whole villages may migrate or have ever migrated in order to avoid a danger announced by a spiritual being through its medium. The following proverb gives substance to this interesting topic: »*Siroota kibula, asengusa ekyalo.*«[12]

Certain physical beings and given phenomena are believed to play a special role in delivering particular messages, a role which earns them their qualifications as peculiar physical beings and special phenomena, respectively.

Consider these examples. A bee, that flies several rounds over the head of a house woman who is preparing a meal, signalizes to that woman the visit of someone who shall share that meal.[13] The cry of the jackal at night[14], the singing of a bird named *nasse-enswa*,[15] the, for the Baganda, strikingly »out of the ordinary singing« of the owl, and the reflex movement of the lower eye-lid are special phenomena by way of which one is fore-warned about a certain sad and impeding situation. Any of those occurrences or phenomena is believed to portend a future bad event, say the death of a relative.

Let us consider for a moment occurrences or phenomena that regard an, so to speak, instantaneous awareness of some truth, which, nonetheless, does not derive from empirical information.

Take the case of a distant labourer working and living far away from his relatives. When such a man loses a relative, he may receive what we call an instinctive feeling that something, somewhere has gone amiss, a feeling that is called »*ekyebikiro*«. But, what is *ekyebikiro?*

---

[12] The literal meaning is: one whose dreams always come true, sets a whole village into migration. Elderly people narrate stories of whole villages migrating in response to, or out of respect for a message from the living-dead about an impeding danger of disease, war, and so on.

[13] Any visit, therefore, that is not, so to speak, signalized by the flying of a bee, is regarded as a very abrupt visit. Consequently, a visitor, whose visit is not announced in above given manner, is welcome, but described thus: »*Omugenyi atazunza njuki*«; that is, he/she is referred to as a visitor who does not »cause« a bee to announce his/her coming.

[14] There is a proverb about this cry of the jackal and its message, thus: »*Ssekisolo ekibuulira abantu: nti abaana b'empisiyisi be bambuulira.*« Ferdinand Walser translates this proverb with words similar to these: the animal, the jackal, that is actually telling the people says, however, that, »the children of the passersby told me.« See Walser, F. Luganda Proverbs. Berlin, 1982, p. 442.

[15] The name literally means, »I killed white ants.«

There are strong claims, among the Baganda, regarding the possibility of transmitting knowledge from one mind to another otherwise than through the channels of the senses. A common form of this means of communication, which however concerns the transmission of bad news, is named »*ekyebikiro.*«

In most cases, such forms of communication are accompanied by special bodily feelings; for example, the twitching of the eye-lid (called *ekisulo*) or a slight fever (named *ekitengo*).

Proverbs as Compendia of Knowledge

The above given notes regarding the problem of knowledge in Baganda Ntu'ology have been guided by constant references to popular epigrams or maxims or idioms, let us call them proverbs. Besides considering them generally as a precious legacy of a philosophizing past, I regard Baganda proverbs as brief summaries of varied fields of knowledge, and, hence, as compendia of knowledge.

Depending on these compendia of knowledge for the greatest part of this chapter, I have presented *amagezi* or knowledge, from the view point of Baganda Ntu'ology, on the one hand, as the direct apprehension of sense data, objects of memory, internal states and of oneself; and, on the other hand, as mediated knowledge of other beings or selves, or as constructs of physical beings.

Chapter seven
Buntu'ology

What is *Buntu'ology?* Generally said, it is a sub-division of Baganda Ntu'ology. By »*Buntu'ology*«, I indicate wisdom that is the basic principle for a classification of reality and values according to the modality category or the *Buntu* category of being. The subject matter of *Buntu'ology* consists of provisions regarding the measure, manner, procedure, form, variety, expression, manifestation, arrangement, pattern of being and values. To be included here are: provisions expressed by means of a variety of themes regarding the modality of being and values, for instance, education, aesthetic values, freedom, responsibility, virtues, vices, norms, knowledge, weight, capacity, length, area, volume, health, character traits, etc.

Buntu'ology and the Problem of Values

Principles or qualities that the Baganda regard as intrinsically valuable or desirable to the *muntu* constitute the basic subject matter of Buntu'ology with regard to the problem of values. The »being intrinsically valuable or desirable« of these principles or qualities depends much, though not exclusively, on their relative worth, utility or importance to the *muntu*.

It appears to me, that the Baganda see the source of value in what I term the »goodness consciousness«. In my phraseology, the goodness consciousness refers to the awareness of the actual or expected goodness or its absence in an object. Consequently, objects are endowed with value through actual or possible goodness consciousness. That is, an object possesses value because it is actually or potentially recognized as good, as possessing goodness. No wonder that, in Luganda, goodness or »*obulungi*« may be attributed to any object that is actually or potentially recognized as good, as possessing goodness.

A highly recognized form of actually or potentially possessing goodness is expressed by the compound term *obuntu-bulamu*, a term which literally signifies a condition of being a healthy human being. The health here in question is not primarily bodily or physical health. It is rather the condition of being morally healthy, the state of possessing moral goodness. Hence, when a person is referred to as *omuntu-mulamu*, it is not principally a reference to a live or healthy person; although this would be the literally derived meaning of that phrase. Rather, *omuntu-mulamu* applies primarily to that person whose conduct abounds in a particular type of *obulungi* or goodness called moral goodness.

Moral Values and Obligations

Moral values receive a bulk of attention in Buntu'ology, since they take precedence over other values. The key reason why values claim a priority with respect to the moral aspect of human experience is to be sought in the role that they play regarding *muntu*'s duty to maintain the ontological harmony of the various realms of the universe.[1]

The principles of morality to which *muntu* appeals to guide him/her in maintaining this harmony, are at once the values or norms or ideals that justify *muntu*'s behaviour. It is in this sense that I hold the view that: morality, in Buntu'ology, has its genesis in *muntu*'s duty to maintain the ontological harmony of the various realms of the universe. Hence, *muntu*'s »moral goodness consciousness«, i.e., his/her awareness of the actual or expected moral goodness or its absence in an object, is based upon the consciousness of his/her duty to maintain the ontological harmony of the various realms of the universe.

Consequently, any act that fosters harmony in the universe is deemed »morally good,« while acts that discompose or interfere with the harmony in the universe are termed morally evil.

No wonder, the Baganda believe that moral evil produces natural

---

[1] *Amaanyi*, as we observed in Chapter Four above, confers unity and harmony to the universe. The three realms of the universe are, for the Baganda, inseparably united and exist in harmony with each other. *Muntu*, who on being born into this universe finds these realms inextricably interwoven, has the duty to maintain this ontological harmony of the universe.

evil, since the former discomposes or interferes with the ontological order of things in the universe. Adultery, for instance, is believed to breed miscarriage[2]. Similarly, popular belief has it that, if a pregnant woman ridicules a cripple, she may give birth to either a lame or a dead child. The causes of natural misfortunes, calamities, disasters, etc. are, generally said, attributed to the immoral acts of evil agents.[3]

To respect the harmony in the universe, as we noted already, is a key duty of every *muntu*. This duty has very significant social features: *muntu* may act as an individual, but the effects of his deeds affect the whole social group. On that matter, consider the proverb: »*Omulya mmamba aba omu, navumaganya ekika*«.[4] The Baganda share with many other Africans this, so to speak, strong social moral »goodness consciousness« that an individual has vis-à-vis his/her social group.[5]

With regard to values, Buntu'ology is not a simple ethical theory but rather concerns itself unvaryingly with both considerations of moral value and considerations of moral obligation. Furthermore, rightness is hereby considered as dependent on or connected in some way with both the goodness or value of action or consequences to the individual, and the goodness or value of action or consequences to his/her social group.

The Ethics of Truth and Falsehood

The Luganda term for truth is *amazima*, and the word obutuufu (i.e., correctness, accuracy) is closely linked in meaning to *amazima*. Several

---

[2] Cf. Roscoe, J. op. cit., p. 350
[3] See also: Mbiti, J. S. Religions, p. 245
[4] Its literal meaning is: It is a single person who eats the prohibited lung-fish; but the whole clan shares the blame.
[5] Some thinkers have misinterpreted this emphasis on the individual's duty to society with respect to moral obligations. What I have called a strong social moral consciousness has led such thinkers to conclude that morality, in the African sense of the word, is simply extrinsic but not intrinsic to the individual. That is, for the African, so such thinkers, moral law can be traced back not to an interior divine law, but to the common good of the group. For further information on that matter see Emefie, I. M. God and Man in African Religion. London, 1981, p. 36
It may also be useful to consider the ideas of Godfrey Parrinder regarding his misinterpretation of the link between social relations and morality. Consider: Parrinder, G. Africa's Three Religions. London, 1969, p. 89

Luganda words express the idea of falsehood, i.e., the absence of truth or accuracy. Consider the following brief list of words: i. *obutanwa;* ii. *okuwubwa;* iii. *ensobi.*[6]

While, in Buntu'ology, acts or conditions that cultivate or further an intentional deviation from truth or accuracy are highly discouraged[7], it is also stressed that truth should serve to maintain the harmony in the universe. The way a piece of truth is communicated, for instance, ought to respect the solidarity, togetherness existing between the different entities in the universe. The ethics of truth and falsehood among the Baganda is, therefore, both fundamentally anthropocentric and basically sociocentric.

The anthropocentric and socio-centric characters of the ethics of truth and falsehood also feature in an express manner in the internal-evidence-process of acquiring truth or true knowledge. The Baganda understanding of obviousness includes, on the one hand, self-consciousness and, on the other hand, the role the spiritual beings play in transmitting knowledge. Section 7.2.4 above indirectly highlighted the point that the spiritual world is actively involved in the human act of knowing the truth. The moral significance of this state of affairs or the moral, the practical lesson to be drawn from this situation of transmitting and acquiring true knowledge is: one ought to exercise a lot of prudence in handling the truth that one knows, otherwise one's act could interfere with the harmony prevailing between beings in both the physical and the spiritual worlds.

Truth also serves to maintain the harmony in the universe when it is explicitly or implicitly employed to abet the cause of moral goodness; that is, when it is used to assist or support in the achievement of a

---

[6] *Obutanwa* indicates a quality or state of being false through unpremeditated means. A slight error caused by inattention, forgetfulness is expressed by the verb *okuwubwa.* Any absence of truth or accuracy, whether it is intentional or due to an act or condition of ignorance is described as *ensobi.*

[7] There is a whole system of, so to speak, moral guidance in regard to truth and falsehood, a system that comprises moral laws, taboos, friendly means of correction through songs, tales or sayings, and so on.
The following proverb is a good example on that matter: »*Wekiina nga ow'ettulu akiika embuga, nti: bakira omwami ayogera nga mmusimbye abiri.*« Literally translated, it means: you are bluffing like a one-eyed person who after visiting the chief's court reports that: »as the chief addressed the public, I had my two eyes fixed on him.«
It is a saying or proverb that discourages telling even the simplest type of lies.

moral purpose. Let us take the example of cases where the external-evidence-process of acquiring and transmitting truth or true knowledge is used to advance the moral virtue of prudence or self-control, cases which the following proverb summarizes thus: »*Ow'ensumattu tasimba bigambo ku mannyo*«.[8] This saying demonstrates how much the Baganda discourage utterances which might be true, but disastrous to the harmonious social relations between people.

A case similar to the foregoing is an instance whereby the authority of an elder – authority which binds a family together – is likely to be challenged by means of a message of truth to be delivered by an inferior person. Without intending to compromise the truth, priority is thereby given to the role of authority in binding people, and not to truth when it separates people.[9]

Buntu'ology stresses on the one hand that truth serves to maintain the harmony in the universe. It emphasises, on the other hand, the point that truth is one. There is in Buntu'ology, therefore, a lot of room for themes or topics like: mendacity, falsity, falsehood, misinterpretation, etc. The reasons for the absence of truth or accuracy may be varied: it could be that the respective individual's intellect and/or senses are not in sound order. It could also be the case that the truth about the respective object is reported wrongly.[10]

Buntu'ology and the Modality Category

I introduced this chapter by defining Buntu'ology as the basic principle for a classification of reality and values according to the modality category or the *Buntu* category of being. However, in the course of the discussion on Buntu'ology, I have dwelt on the problem of values, since

---

[8] That is: an inconsiderate talkative person does not keep back his/her words.
[9] The relative phrase, »*omukulu tasobya*« (an elder does not err or stray) is, for instance, never used to exhibit how infallible the elders are, but rather it is employed to warn the younger party who tries to challenge an elder unnecessarily.
Consider, too, this related saying: »*Nnyini mwana akubuulira: nti omwana yambuulira*« (the parent is informing you; and you say, the child told me!).
[10] These two proverbs are material for thought about that matter: *Tekiwoomera matama abiri* (something can hardly have the same taste to two different mouths); and, *N'omugezi awubwa: amatu tegawulira vvumbe*« (An intelligent person, too, can be mistaken; moreover, ears are not capable of smelling).

this question or problem is the dominant, though not exclusive, theme in Buntu'ology.

Any study of the classification of reality and values according to the modality category or the *Buntu* category of being incorporates discussions on a variety of topics, ranging from very practical to highly theoretical themes. The amount that a thing weighs *(buzito)*, the quality or state of being short *(bumpi)*, the extent of elevation above a level, or the extent of depth below a level, or the condition of being tall or high *(buwanvu)*, the distance from side to side *(bugazi)*, the cubic capacity of something or the space measure in cubic units *(bwagagavu)*, the state or quality of being copious *(bungi)*, etc. are some of the themes on practical matters, themes that are also addressed by Buntu'ology.

Topics like, the comprehensive quality of learning or knowing *(bugezi)*, any characteristic and oft-times unconscious mode *(embeera)* or peculiarity of action, bearing, or treatment, and other related themes, also number among the questions treated in Buntu'ology.

Chapter eight
Muntu-Muntu Relationship

Subsequent to sections of this study that have demonstrated in brief who and/or what the *muntu* is, what and/or how he/she knows other NTU, and, too, how *muntu* classifies reality and values according to the Buntu category, is yet another chapter that intends to highlight further the phenomenon of concentrating awareness and understanding of reality and values about the human being, a phenomenon that I have named »Muntu-centrism.«

Muntu, the Relational Being

A very significant element of *muntu's* being is, as we pointed out in Chapter Five above, »being in relation to«. *Muntu* and the other beings in the universe are constantly in interaction with each other. In Baganda Ntu'ology, *muntu* is hence conceived as a being that is interwoven in a network of relations with other beings. That is, *muntu* is a relational being. He/she stands constantly in relationship with *Katonda*, the creator and supreme being, with *balubaale, mayembe, misambwa* and *mizimu*, the spiritual beings, with his/her living and dead clan or family members, with his/her piece of land and domestic animals, etc.

To be in relation to other NTU is of such crucial importance for the being of any individual *muntu*, that, on the one hand, his/her »not being in relation to« other NTU is equivalent in effect to his/her ceasing to be or, eventually, to his/her not-being. On the other hand, the more a particular human being succeeds in cultivating and maintaining a good sense of belonging, good relationships with other NTU, the higher his/her status as *omuntu-mulamu*[1] gets, the more he/she is a live person.

---

[1] For further information on *omuntu-mulamu*, see Chapter Seven, above.

It is from this perspective of *muntu* as a relational being, that we shall consider, in subsequent sections of this chapter, a particular *muntu*'s »being in relation to« another *muntu*.

Muntu, the Community Man/Woman

The clause, »the more a particular human being succeeds in cultivating and maintaining a good sense of belonging, the higher his/her status as *omuntu-mulamu,* as a live person is«, does not barely lay an accent on *muntu*'s relational beingness, but it points to the fact that he/she lives in an interacting population of beings of his species, i.e. *bantu*.[2] It is afterall these other *bantu* who create for the individual the social occasion, the social background against which the respective individual is able to see himself/herself as *omuntu-mulamu.*

For the Baganda it might be easy to conceive of an individual person being lonely, living alone on some island. But, even in such cases that person is not conceived as an isolated individual. A live *muntu* always lives in the community of either both the living and the living-dead, or barely in intimate fellowship with the living-dead, say in the case whereby one lives alone as a human being on an island.

It is within the community circumstances or community life shared with other *bantu* that the individual *muntu* realizes most concretely his/her relational »beingness.« It is there that he/she sees himself/herself as embedded in a network of social and kinship relationships: he/she knows himself/herself not simply as a being existing »in relation to« other beings, but also as a friend of so and so, as a neighbour, a son/daughter, a father/mother, etc.

The community hence concretizes *muntu*'s relational »beingness.« It grants him/her a concrete status as a relational being. His/her identity is solidified and advertised by the social identity of his/her community. To re-phrase the well-known words of J. S. Mbiti: »*Muntu* is because *Bantu* are, and since *Bantu* are therefore *muntu* is« (the original version: »I am because we are, and since we are therefore I am«). I am, for instance, a father/mother because we are a family, or since we form a village, I am the neighbour of somebody.

---

[2] At this juncture, one is reminded that *bantu* (persons, people), is the plural form of *muntu*.

Beyond meaning »belonging to a social or kinship group«, *muntu's* being in the community means for the Baganda, like it does for many other Africans, »being implanted in the community« as if by roots of a living organism. Hence a community in Baganda Ntu'ology is a unity of dynamic relational beings, and not a unit or association of atomic individuals.

The Macro »Bundle« of Relational Beings

A community in Baganda Ntu'ology has been described as a unity of dynamic relational beings. Referring to small communities of *bantu*, say the family or clan, I may re-phrase this description thus: a community is a micro unity of relational beings. This description applies mutatis mutandis to a larger community of *bantu*, e.g. the ethnic group called the Baganda. It is in this sense that I understand the Baganda, a conglomerate of families and clans, as a *macro* unity of relational beings. This section intends to outline the socio-political theory and practice that underlie the macro unity of relational beings called the Baganda.

»Omuganda«, the Analogy of the Bundle

History narrates that the first settlers in the present-day region called Buganda[3] and the later group that came from Southern Ethiopia to co-inhabit that land[4], seem to have been related to each other. Among the chiefs or elders in the latter group was a very able leader, later King Kintu, who organised the different clans into a single people, as if into a »bundle« or »*omuganda*«.[5]

In the first Chapter of this study, we observed that the words »*muganda*« and »*baganda*« stem from the word »*omuganda*« meaning »a bundle«, signifying unity, and suggesting a common ancestry, a kin-

---

[3] Quite little is known about the origins of these first settlers, »*Abalasangeye*«. It would appear, however, that as they came into this region, they found the land uninhabited and hence called it »Muwawa«, i.e. a narrow, uninhabited piece of land. On that matter, consider Kyewalyanga, F. X. op. cit. p. 9
[4] For further information on this migration, see, especially: Ibidem.
[5] Consider Ddiba, J. L. Eddiini mu Buganda, Kitovu, 1955, p. 18

ship or a certain degree of blood relationship that binds or ought to bind the Baganda together. Against the background of the analogy of the bundle, I wish to refer to the Baganda as a »macro bundle of relational beings«, to mean, nonetheless, the same thing as what I explained already, above. That is, the Baganda are a macro unity of relational beings.

»Oluganda«, the Bundling-Principle[6]

The basic principle for the process of »bundling the Baganda«[7], a principle that permitted the founding members of the Baganda tribe to draw an analogy between the people or *abantu* and a group of things that are fastened together for convenient handling or a bundle, has to be sought within the context of an element, a character or a quality shared by both the Baganda and a bundle.

To my contention, the basic principle for the process of »bundling the Baganda« is »*oluganda*«. In the context of »bundling the Baganda«, *oluganda* is a fundamental principle that is the character or quality of a whole made up of intimately associated individuals, elements, or parts. This character or quality is expressed in the unity, integrity and solidarity prevailing among the parts or elements or individuals of that whole.

Studying the accounts regarding the process of social cohesion of the two groups that occupied Buganda as their place of settled residence, one gets an impression of a peaceful course of events. More so, one notes that both groups seem to have been related to each other long before they joined residence in Buganda. I am inclined to think that, in the process of social cohesion between the two groups, the original »bundling of the Baganda« was effected, first and foremost, by *oluganda*, the »bundling-principle«. The question is: How could this bundling or unity have been achieved?

---

[6] Regarding *oluganda,* see also Chapter One, above.
[7] The self-coined phrase »bundling the Baganda« is constructed against the background of both the above-given notes on the analogy of the bundle and, as well, the meaning of the verb or noun »bundle«; that is, the »making of things into a bundle or package«.
The phrase, »bundling the Baganda« is therefore intended to refer to the practice of bringing or holding the Baganda together as a tribe, whether in the past or in the present times.

The proposal that, »both groups seem to have been related to each other« suggests to me that they spoke the same language or similar dialects. Accordingly, *olugunda*, to mean, in the first instance, »the language spoken by the Baganda«, helped these people to overcome the key natural or human barrier of social cohesion; namely, that of verbal communication. In the second instance, the impression »that both groups seem to have been related to each other« leads me to suppose that in the course of relating verbally with each other, both groups found out that they had the same or similar stories about their origins. This would further allude to a common ancestry, a kinship or a certain degree of blood relationship.

Consequently, *oluganda*, the bundling-principle for the Baganda is, firstly that law of unity that bundles by breaking down the barriers of human communication, especially the barriers of verbal communication. Secondly, *oluganda* is that precept that bundles through indicating or suggesting a common ancestry, a kinship or a certain degree of blood relationship.

»Abaganda«, the Material for Bundling

In the context of the above said, the material for the practice or action of bundling are the people themselves. The fact that the Baganda or *Abaganda* as a social group are divided into three classes may appear to suggest a disuniting system or process of rigid social stratification among the Baganda, a system that is akin to »casteism.« In such a case, the three classes would be in conformity with the principle of »divide and rule.«

However, since all of these people together, regardless of the class to which the one or the other belongs, form one bundle, *omuganda*, the fact of the three classes has to be accepted as a method of assemblage for better bundling. The underlying principle is therefore, not »divide and rule«, but rather, »bunch up and bundle.« The three classes of *Abaganda* are: *abalangira, abakungu,* and *abakopi*.[8]

---

[8] *Abalangira*, singular *omulangira*, means the princes. As a class of people it refers to the royal family *(olulyo olulangira)*, and hence includes, too, the princesses *(abambejja)*. *Abakungu*, singular *omukungu*, refers mainly to high ranking chiefs and ministers of the King, *Kabaka*.

»Obuganda«, the Binding Force or System

Regarding the unity of the Baganda, I have portrayed *oluganda* as the »bundling-principle«, as a fundamental principle that is the character or quality of a whole made up of intimately associated individuals, elements, or parts. This fundamental principle is translated into practice by means of a system or by the help of a binding force. I consider what is called »*obuganda*« to be this binding force or system.

In the general sense of the word, *obuganda* means, the Kingdom of Buganda. Consider the common saying: »*Obuganda buladde*«; that is, *obuganda* is calm. The actual meaning of this often loud eager expression of praise or approval is: the Kingdom of Buganda is in a state of repose and freedom from wars and turmoil; it is at peace internally and with its neighbours. Such a state of affairs presupposes unity among the Baganda, unity which is guaranteed by the efficient and efficacious functioning of, first of all, the political organs and structures. In the political organization of Buganda, the *Kabaka* (King) is assisted by the *Katikkiro* (the Prime-Minister), *Ab'amasaza* (county chiefs), *Ab'amagombolola* (sub-county chiefs), *Ab'emiruka* (parish chiefs) and *Abatongole* (village chiefs).

Secondly, unity among the Baganda is guaranteed by the figure of the King. The King is called *Kabaka*, a name that bears a lot of historical notes. The first King of the Baganda, Kintu, was respected as a saviour of Buganda, since he united the various clans into one tribe. He was regarded as an ambassador from heaven,[9] a man with divine powers; hence, the title »Kabaka«, which originates from the word »*omubaka*«, meaning a messenger or an ambassador. Ever since, Kabaka, the King, is regarded as an ambassador of God who rules by divine decree.[10] The King, then, plays a key role of uniting the human beings among themselves, as well as, the duty of uniting them with the beings in the spiritual world.

In the narrower sense of the word, *obuganda* means, one's being a

---

Abakopi, singular *omukopi*, are the commoners, a group that includes mainly the peasants.

[9] The Baganda »Genesis of the Human Being Story« narrates the direct link that Kintu had with »*Ggulu*«, heaven.

[10] For further details concerning *Kabaka*'s role in uniting the physical world of the human beings with the spiritual world of the spirits, consider the explanation offered in Chapter Four, above.

member of the Baganda ethnic group, i. e. being *omuganda*. As we observed above, with respect to the *muntu* as a community being, *muntu*, in Baganda Ntu'ology, has no existence outside the community. *Muntu* needs the community to be conscious of what he/she is as an individual being. Consequently, an individual's being *omuganda* is at once the Baganda social order as lived in his/her family and in his/her clan. The following elaboration on the significance of the clan among the Baganda also demonstrates how unity among the Baganda is guaranteed by the clan system.

The Luganda word for the clan is »*ekika*«. *Ekika* (plural, *ebika)* has its etymological roots in the basic root »*ka*«; that is, the basic root for the variants of the word which means home or family. It would appear that *ekika* originally meant the residence, the home or seat of any given group of (blood) relatives. *Ekika* has therefore the fundamental meaning of that basic home in which one exists as *omuganda*. It is alternatively that basic home outside which there is no existence as *omuganda*.

The basic home, *ekika*, is organised as follows: the individual, *omuntu*, is attached by birth to a household *(enda)*; the household is bound by blood relationship to an extended family *(enju)*; the extended family is further attached by blood relationship to a lineage *(olunyiriri)*; the lineage is part of a sub-clan *(omutuba)*; and the sub-clan is subdivision of the clan acme *(akasolya)*.

The authors B. Radcliffe and friends consider the role the clans play, with respect to establishing unity among the Baganda, to consist in the convergence of interests and sentiments, as well as in controlling, avoiding and limiting conflicts which arise as a result of divergence in sentiments and interests.[11]

In summary, the fundamental principle for the unity of the Baganda, i. e., *oluganda* is translated into practice by means of *obuganda* or a binding system, a binding force. *Obuganda* is achieved and furthered by the political system, the distinctive intermediary role of the *Kabaka* and by the clan system.

---

[11] Cf. Radcliffe, B., et. al., ed. African Systems of Kinship and Marriage. London, 1975, p. 3.

»Emizizo«, the Binding Codes

The Luganda word *emizizo*, singular *omuzizo*, refers to protective measures or prohibitions imposed by Baganda social customs and laws. *Emizizo* are instruments of preserving peace and harmony in society. They encompass all areas and walks of the Baganda social and private life.[12] As we noted in the previous chapter, every individual *muntu* has the duty of maintaining harmony in the universe. Since one of the features of this harmony in the universe is the unity prevailing among the various members of the Baganda ethnic group, every individual *muntu* has the duty of maintaining this unity, say by adhering to *emizizo* or by binding oneself to observance of *emizizo*.

Hence, in this context of preserving harmony in the universe or maintaining unity among the Baganda, *emizizo* are reminders about the necessity of doing what promotes peace, harmony and unity in society. They are, as well, binding suggestions about the necessity of not doing what interferes with peace, harmony and unity in society.

In the foregoing sections, we observed that the more a particular human being succeeds in preserving or promoting peace, harmony and unity in society, say through cultivating and maintaining a good sense of belonging, good relationships with other NTU, the higher his/her status as *omuntu-mulamu* gets, the more he/she is a live person. Conversely, interfering with peace, harmony and unity in society lessens one's status as *omuntu-mulamu* or one's standing as a socially live person.

In connection with the issue of increasing or lessening one's standing as a socially live person, *emizizo* also serve the purpose of maintaining or re-establishing the normal level of social and/or individual life which is often lessened by interfering with peace, harmony and unity in society.

The impact of *emizizo* as binding codes for peace, harmony and unity in society is felt mostly when there is a grievous infraction or violation of any of them. Disputes arising from breaching *emizizo* are dealt with by elders or sages, ranging from heads of families to the King himself.[13]

---

[12] Consider Mpuuga, W. Amagezi g'abedda. Kampala, 1976, pp. 5ff
[13] For further information on this matter, see especially, Kaggwa, A. Ekitabo ky'Empisa z'Abaganda. Kampala, 1918, pp. 238–246.

Aspect three   Muntu-centrism in Baganda Ntu'ology

The antecedent elaboration on the *muntu-muntu* relationship leads us to the conclusion that: the conceptual picture of *muntu* is incomplete without the notion of a shared existence, that is, the notion of muntu as relational being or a community man/woman or a part of the »bundle« of relational beings. In Baganda Ntu'ology, then, *muntu* as an individual exists because others exist. On the contrary, *muntu* does not exist, – to follow the Cartesian principle of »cogito, ergo sum« –, barely because he/she thinks.

Chapter nine
Muntu and Deity

The following conceptual picture of *muntu* was portrayed in Chapter Five above: he/she is a being living in a universe permeated with *amaanyi*, the all-reality-permeating dynamism, the immanence of the spiritual in the material. The previous chapter has, in its turn, emphasized the relational beingness of *muntu*. Accordingly, *muntu* is both a being that constantly interacts with other beings in the physical and spiritual worlds, as well as a being that »lives« with the one whom he/she reveres and exalts as supremely good and powerful. Let us attempt a close look at *muntu's* relationship with deity, with »the one whom he/she reveres and exalts as supremely good and powerful«.

Relating to »Kyetondeka«

The Baganda, like other Africans, are not only deeply religious but live in a world which they regard as religious.[1] The world is perceived as religious, since it is permeated with *amaanyi*. The ultimate source and guide to *amaanyi* is »the one whom muntu reveres and exalts as supremely good and powerful«. The Baganda expose their understanding of, and relationship with the Supreme Being in a variety of ways: in religious rituals and ceremonies, in myths, folk-tales and fables, in names, prayers, songs, proverbs, etc.

A very old song tells of who and/or what the Supreme Being is for the Baganda. Considered the following verse of that song: »... *Zaali bbiri okuzaala akaliga, ani yakazaala, Kyetondeka, akatooke e*

---

[1] Besides directing our attention to Chapter Four above, we may further refer to the authors, Timothy M. Ssemogerere and John Roscoe, who likewise affirm that the Baganda are notoriously religious. Consider: Ssemogerere, T. M., ed., Katekismu ya Mapeera Kampala, 1983, 257; and Roscoe, J. op. cit., p. 271

Mbale ...« Literally translated, the verse means: »... there were two (sheep) to bear a lamb; (but) who actually brought forth the lamb, one who set himself firmly, like a banana tree at Mbale.«[2]

The above given verse inquires into the ultimate origin of a lamb. In proposing that it was *Kyetondeka* who is ultimately responsible for that action, it provides an illustrated clarification regarding the »search for an ultimate explanation« about that particular instance. Let us examine the phraseology more closely.

The words »... *zaali bbiri* ...«, mean. »there were two (sheep) ...« The third person plural demonstrative pronoun »*zaali*« designates animals and things rather than human or supra-human beings. Hence, reference is hereby made to animals (sheep), and but not to a human being nor to a super-human being.

The phrase »... *ani yakazaala* ...«, means: »who gave birth to the lamb ...« One notes that the verse no longer addresses the parent-sheep; far beyond that, it now ponders the possibility of another contributory hand in the birth-story of the lamb. This is expressly illustrated by the use of the interrogative word »*ani*« (who), which alludes to a human or supra-human being rather than to a thing or an animal. That is, all of a sudden, the accent changes from »two sheep giving birth to a lamb« to »another being bearing the responsibility for the birth of the lamb«, a being that supersedes the level of animals.

The word *Kyetondeka* means: »one who set himself firmly«, »one who fixed himself solidly«. *Kyetondeka* is likened to a banana tree that sets itself definitely and even flourishes in a semi-desert location as if by a miracle. That implies that *Kyetondeka* is »that which, or one who flourishes without the contribution of *muntu*«.

In the context of the above given birth-story of the lamb, *muntu* submits, so to speak, his/her null contribution to the respective circumstances. I may put it sardonically thus: *muntu* responds to the question, »... *ani yakazaala?*« (who ultimately brought forth the lamb?«) with the answer: »It was *Kyetondeka*, and not I«. Consequently, *muntu* con-

---

[2] Mbale is a village in Mawokota County in Buganda. It is a semi-arid area with unsuitable conditions for the growth of banana trees. In several songs, Mbale is presented as a semi-desert area, where a banana tree can never flourish, let alone, the attempt, to plant it. In such a context, it would not only be a miracle to find a banana tree thriving in Mbale, but such a plant »must have fixed itself«, since nobody would waste their time on such an undertaking.

fesses his/her inability vis-à-vis *Kyetondeka's* ability in two aspects. That is, besides admitting his/her null contribution to the birth of the lamb, he/she also confesses that lack of sufficient personal and immediate experience or sufficient direct knowledge about the respective circumstances. On the contrary, *Kyetondeka* does not only abundantly and directly know the circumstances surrounding the birth of the lamb, but he is responsible for its existence.

In a similar manner, the Baganda consider the »one who set or fixed himself firmly« to have direct knowledge about the circumstances surrounding the origin of the universe. They also regard him to be responsible for its continual existence and sustenance. Like his name suggests, Kyetondeka has no origin. No one knows whence he came to fix himself firmly into the universe. More still, corresponding to his works, is the nature of his being: he is an all-knowing and all-powerful being; he is also benevolent and just.

Relating to »Katonda«

Kyetondeka has several other names. Most significant among those names or attributes is, *Katonda*, the creator.[3] *Katonda*[4] is at once the name or attribute of a deity, and an expression of the highest rank or highest essential nature of a good. He is distinguished from the minor deities by the qualification »*Katonda w'e Butonda*«.[5] Despite being »the one whom *muntu* reveres and exalts as supremely good and powerful«, *Katonda* is approachable, as the following elaboration demonstrates.

His sanctuary is the whole hill *Butonda* in Buganda. It is his palace on earth. *Butonda* ought to reflect in a visible manner how immanent *Katonda* can be. There is no shrine at *Butonda*. The absence of a specific point as the sanctuary of *Katonda* at *Butonda* marks the Baganda's relationship with him as different from their interaction with the minor deities. Any *Muganda,* any member of the Baganda tribe, irrespec-

---

[3] Regarding Katonda, see, also Chapter Five above, especially, Section 5.1.4
[4] John Samuel Mbiti describes »Katonda« as the most ancient name of God commonest to the Baganda. On that matter, see Mbiti, J. S. concepts, p. 47.
[5] On Katonda w'e Butonda, consider, too: Kyewalyanga, F. X. op. cit., p. 99.

tive of his/her clan membership, may approach *Katonda* without the assistance of a medium. Moreover, acts of offering something precious to a deity, say the killing of an animal on an altar, are unknown at *Butonda hill*. This means, *Katonda* may receive donations; he does not demand sacrifices, however.

Hence, *Katonda* is propitiously transcendent, because he is »the one whom *muntu* reveres and exalts as supremely good and powerful«. He is also benignly immanent, since he is *Katonda w'e Butonda (the God of Butonda hill)*.

Naming God, Praying to God

The *muntu-deity* relationship is further highlighted by the phenomenon of naming God. One notes that the words or phrases employed in naming God constitute, in most of the cases, distinctive designations of, so to say, a personalized deity. According to my observation, most of the Baganda names for God make or convey an impression of distinctive designations of a »super-human person.« This observation may impart additional substance onto my above given position that the Baganda regard God to be is propitiously transcendent, and, too, benignly immanent.

God is *Kyetondeka* (one who fixed himself solidly) and *Katonda* (the creator), as mentioned above. He is also called by distinctive titles that allude to practical skills or manual arts: he is *Namugereka* (one who correctly determines shapes or adjusts things), *Kawamigero* (one who ascertains »weights and measures«), *Bugingo* (one who creates with dexterity or skill) and *Namugeta* (one who is skilful).

The Baganda give God descriptive names that express their notion of God's nature: he is, for instance, metaphorically titled *Ssemanda* (the master of charcoal). Like a craftsman who employs charcoal-heat to melt or break or join metals in order to form new devices out of them, so does God have unlimited power over all the beings in the universe. He may do with them what he wills. God is also »one who possesses all things« (Ssebintu).

The compound name *Liiso-ddene*, too, expresses the Baganda's notion of God's nature. *Liiso-ddene* literally denotes a »big eye«. Its use as a name of God suggests a likeness between the faculty of seeing and God's ability, to put it literally, to see everything. This name, as

John Samuel Mbiti understands it, is employed as a metaphor to express God's omniscience.[6] The omniscient God is also eternal, as the name Ssewannaku (king of days) illustrates.

The one who created the universe *(Katonda)*, possesses all things *(Ssebintu)*, provides for his creation. He is therefore named *Kagaba* or *Lugaba* (one who causes others to have or receive); and *Ddunda* (the shepherd or pastor).

Where does God abide? According to Baganda Ntu'ology or specifically according to Wantu'ology, God's home is found in the »upwardness« (waggulu) of the earth. No wonder, his name *Ggulu* literally means heaven. Besides being merely *Ggulu*, he is also *Sseggulu* (master of heaven).

The constant use of the masculine personal pronoun »he« in reference to God in this sub-section is not a *lapsus calamae*. Rather, it demonstrates the fact the Baganda consider God to be a man. I am inclined to think that they regard God to be a male being, since they trace descent through the paternal line; that is, they are a patrilineal society.

One would certainly search in vain for a name by means of which the Baganda offer a definition of God. The above given and the rest of the Baganda names of God express a conception of the qualities, attributes of God. These names are, therefore, descriptions and not definitions of God. These names are, on the one hand, descriptions regarding the nature of God; on the other hand, they express *muntu's* contingency, as well as his dependence on God.

Muntu's contingency and his/her dependence on God are also declared by the prayers. It is my observation and a notice worthy point that prayer, in Baganda Ntu'ology, is mainly an individual or group socio-psychological position with regard to facts or states of affairs that indicate *muntu's* dependence on God.

Prayers are expressed in peoples' names, in greetings and salutations, in blessings, proverbs, verbal spiritual invocations, etc.[7] Prayers that take the form of verbal spiritual invocations are, in most of the

---

[6] Consider: Mbiti, J. S. Concepts, p. 2
[7] Consider these examples of what I may term »veiled Baganda prayers«.
i. The personal name Kyalimpa, means, »whatever he (God) will offers me«
ii. The farewell verse Katonda akuume, implies the wish: »let God guard you«;
iii. The proverb Kyaterekera omulamu, tekivunda, may be translated as: »what God destines for the living cannot rot away.«

cases, petition-oriented in nature and exhibit the belief of the Baganda that *muntu* is dependent on God. No wonder, then that such petitions often regard health, wealth, good harvests, fertility of fields and of persons, etc.[8] More so, prayers are not items on the individual's or group's list of programmed activities for the day, week, month or year. Prayer is a continuous awareness of *muntu's* dependence on God; it cannot be strictly programmed or fixed onto a time-table.

An example of a typical Baganda prayer has been translated as follows: »creator (Katonda)! The omnipotent (Nantalemwa)! May you keep our people in good health, and make them prosperous. Let our wives produce children. May our crops and animals increase in number so that we may sacrifice to you crops and animals and not children. May you protect us from our enemies and any sort of danger so that everybody may be at peace and happiness.«[9]

Katonda! Then, whence Evil?

The question is: how do the Baganda account for the fact of evil in the world, whereas they revere and exalt *Katonda* as supremely good and powerful? The belief of the Baganda in *Katonda's* benevolence and power in the face of evil is asserted by the name *Nantayombooza* (the just parent, who loves and cares for all). If *Katonda,* who as a parent, is just and benevolent, then *Katonda* cannot be the cause of evil in the world. For the Baganda, however, evil has a cause, a cause which, nevertheless, roots neither in *Katonda's* nature, nor in his lacking the qualities required for an effective action against evil. In this connection, too, the idea of God letting the human being suffer evil in order to attain something good is odd to Baganda Ntu'ology.

In the Baganda story regarding the genesis of the human being

---

[8] Adeyemo Tokumboh supports this position, thus: »Since the majority of African peoples hail from and live in farming communities, rain, fertility, plenty and health are prime awareness of God's providence for them. Petitioning God for rain is therefore the main objective for many prayers and sacrifices. Different people in Africa acknowledge the sustaining and preserving work of God in various ways. Many consider God to be their keeper, guardian, protector and preserver.« Cf.: Tokumboh, A. Salvation in African Tradition Nairobi, 1979, p. 23.

[9] Waliggo, J. M. »Incarnating Christianity in Uganda.« In: Proceedings of the Second National Theological Week. Katigondo, 1983, p. 113.

and the origin of the arch-evil, death, it is the human being who is held accountable for introducing evil (death) into the world.[10] Moreover, the human being is in a position to manipulate the power of the spiritual beings for his/her benefit. This power of the spiritual beings may be utilized skilfully by particular human beings to cause good or inflict evil on other beings, including other human beings.[11]

The cause of evil in the world has to be sought in the direct or indirect mal-practices of *muntu*. The Baganda, so to speak, exempt *Katonda* from being party with evil. They even invoke his name for protection against evil, or at least hope for his consolation after experiencing evil.[12]

---

[10] In the »Story of Kintu and Nambi«, the deity Ggulu (the father of Nambi) attempts to hinder Walumbe (death) from following his sister Nambi (the mother of all Baganda) to the earth. Nambi distorts this plan.
For further information on this matter, see, especially, Roscoe, J. op.cit. pp. 460ff.
[11] Ibidem, p. 300ff
[12] To follow is a typical expression of hope in Katonda's consolation: »Katonda omukozi w'ebirungi y'anaddaabiriza balubaale bye bakoze.« That is: it is God, the benevolent one, who will fill up the gaps of evil caused by the evil spirits.

Chapter ten
Death and Destiny

Does death cause *muntu* to cease to exist? Is *muntu* annihilated at his/her death? Why do the Baganda employ the same term, »*omuzimu*«, for the non-material dimension of the living human being, as well as for the spiritual beings of the Kintu category, the spiritual *bintu*? In other words, why does the word *omuzimu* mean both the spiritual element of the living human being, and ordinary spirits or ghosts?

When Muntu Dies ...

According to Baganda Ntu'ology, *omuzimu*, the non-material element of the living human being, deserts the body at the moment of *muntu*'s death. We noted in Chapter Six above, that death is equated with the loss of breath or *omukka*; that is, the moment *omukka* is interrupted, the living human body or *omubiri* becomes a dead body or *omulambo*. Like *omuzimu* deserts the body at death, so disappears the visible manifestation of that non-material element of the living human being or *ekisikirize*, too. That is, the Baganda believe that the life-less body or *omulambo* cannot cast a shadow or *ekisikirize*, not even under the brightest sunshine.

At death, *omuzimu* becomes united with other beings in the spiritual world of the ancestors, the world of the living-dead. The simplest way of describing this change in the mode of being is by saying: he/she has become wind or *empewo*. After joining the world of the ancestors, *muntu*, so to speak, loses his his/her *muntu*ness. He/she no longer belongs to the *Muntu* category of beings, but to the *Kintu* category of existents.

Whereas they speak about *muntu* joining the spiritual world of the ancestors at death, the Baganda, it would appear to me, do not believe in an ultimate separation of the body *(omubiri)* and the spirit *(omuzimu)*. Right from the moment of the death a human being, the Baganda assign *akaba*, the lower jaw-bone a special character. To die is, for instance, also referred to as *okusuula akaba*, i.e., literally, »to let or cause the lower jaw-bone drop.« Moreover, *omuzimu* is believed to cling »forever and wherever« to the lower jaw-bone or *akaba*.[1]

Given burial rites and practices may also give substance to my point of view that, the Baganda do not believe in an ultimate separation of the body *(omubiri)* and the spirit *(omuzimu)*. The following proverb, for instance, partly explains why the dead are wrapped in bark-cloth[2] before burial: »*Atamanyi mpewo y'emagombe, yamma omufu olubugo*.« That is, literally: »one who has no experience of the coldness in the underworld fails or refuses to offer the dead person a piece of bark-cloth.« Moreover, there are instances of some people who are buried with personal belongings, e.g. utensils, articles which are, as it is said, for use in their new life. The history of Buganda has it that some Kings were buried with their (then live) wives and attendants to keep them company in the new world.

On Death

Two Luganda words are frequently used in reference to death; that is, the noun *olumbe* (which also means disease), and the verb *okufa* (which means »to die«). The noun *olumbe* is akin in origin and meaning to the verb *okulumba* which indicates the act of attacking or invading. Death connotes, therefore, that which sets itself upon *muntu* forcefully, or that which affects the human being injuriously. In the most significant of the Baganda myths regarding the origin of death, death is presented as an invader or that which entered the physical world to conquer or plunder human existence.[3] As an invader, death also disrupts human relations, it separates *muntu* from his/her fellow human beings. Hence, the dead person is also named *omugenzi*, »one who is gone,« one who has been separated from the living.

The intransitive verb *okufa*, meaning to die, is essentially related

---

[1] See also, Lugira, M. A. op. cit., p. 109; and Tempels, P. op. cit., p. 37
[2] It is the cherished traditional practice of the Baganda, to wrap their death in bark-cloth before burial.
[3] Reference is hereby made to Chapter Nine above, especially to Footnote 10.

Aspect three   Muntu-centrism in Baganda Ntu'ology

to the transitive verb *okufuula* (to change or transform), and to *okufuuka* (to transform one's the state of being), another intransitive verb. Viewed from the perspective of the meanings of these two verbs, death serves as the mark for a radical transformation, a fundamental alteration of the state or mode being of *muntu*. The following common saying may substantiate this interpretation: »*Walumbe tatta, atereka buteresi.*« That means: the deity of death, *Walumbe*, does not kill; rather, he simply stows away. Accruing from that interpretation, too, is an answer to some questions posed at the beginning of the chapter: death does not cause *muntu* to cease to exist; that is, *muntu* is not annihilated at his/her death.

To my contention, the Baganda notion of death is a concurrent conceptual position. That is, the Baganda hold death to be an occurrence that one »acknowledges, but repudiates« at the same time. What I am presenting here is the strikingly anomalous opposition of ideas, concepts, thoughts, notions, impressions, conceptions about death inherent in Baganda Ntu'ology. Consider the subsequent pair of opposite positions on death.

Instance:
a) Position: »Death is a universal and an inevitable organic process.«
b) Backing: i. The proverb: »*Ssekiriba kya ttaka, mpaawo atalikyambala*«. Literally: nobody ever escapes wearing the skin of the soil; that is, nobody is exempted from going to the grave or from dying.
ii. The saying: »*Olumbe lubugo, tulwesibye*«. That is, death is a bark-cloth which is wrapped around each one of us.

Opposite Instance:
a) Position: »Every death must have a beyond-the-physical-cause cause«.
b) Backing: i. The saying: »*Omuganda*[4] teyefiira«. That means, a human being does not barely die due to physical causes.

---

[4] Beyond the common meaning of this word, *omuganda* means, in this context, *omuntu*, the human being in general.

ii. The general mind of the Baganda on death: the frequent beyond-the-physical-cause causes of death are: the wrath of the spirits of one's deceased relatives, especially the spirit of one's paternal aunt[5]; sorcery or witchcraft; a curse, particularly the curse of one's father, mother or paternal aunt; and, cheating or stealing which involves or results into murder.[6]

With respect to the above given or similar instances, one notices that what I have called opposite positions on death *are* either so far apart as to be irreconcilable, i. e., they are in complete antagonism; or they *seem* so far apart as to be irreconcilable, i. e. they are in sharp contrast. It would however be an exaggeration to call these opposite points of view contradictions, since they do not so completely negate each other that if one is true or valid the other must be false or invalid. At the most, these opposite points of view may be in complete antagonism. In such an extreme condition, they may then be regarded as contrary views, since they imply extreme divergence. They are, even in the case of extreme divergence, not contradictory points of view, however.

The Afterlife

Generally said, the living dead, so the Baganda, go to an »underworld location« called *Magombe*. *Magombe* is described as a very cold place[7], a location of utmost inactivity.[8] In a popular song, *Magombe* is presented as »a place where sweet potatoes cannot grow;«[9] it is, hence, a place devoid of life or any vital activity. I am of the mind that, when the Baganda talk of the dead »going to *Magombe*, they refer to the destiny

---

[5] Cf. Kyewalyanga, F. X. op. cit., p. 81
[6] See Kaggwa, A. op. cit., p. 198
[7] For the sake of additional clarity on this matter, consider again the proverb:»*Atamanyi mpewo y'emagombe, yamma omufu olubugo.*« That is, literally: »one who has no experience of the coldness in the underworld fails or refuses to offer the dead person a piece of bark-cloth.«
[8] Hence, *Magombe* is also called *Zirakumwa*, i. e., a place where even the simple act of shaving cannot be carried out.
[9] That is, »... *emagombe terimwa lumonde* ...«

of *omubiri* (the living human body) which turns into *omulambo* (the dead human body) at death. It is *omulambo*, the material element of the human being, which goes to *Magombe* after burial. I am bent to think like this, since there is talk about another destiny of *muntu* after his/her death.

In line with the above given position, I hold that the talk about yet another destiny of *muntu* after his/her death concerns the after-death-fate of the non-material element of the human being, i.e. *omuzimu*. The point here in question is the entry into the world of the ancestors. There is, nonetheless, no automatic entry into the world of the ancestors. »A visit« to a place called Ttanda precedes acquiring the right or privilege of entering the world of the ancestors. At Ttanda, the dead person has to account for all his/her moral or immoral deeds. If that individual has lived morally and in an harmonious relationship with the other beings in the universe, he/she is raised or promoted to the order or rank or category or class of an ancestor, i.e., to the rank of *lubaale*; otherwise, he/she is banished to world of the evil spirits, i.e. he/she endures the rank of *omuzimu*.[10]

The Foreverness of »Being in Relation to«

Several sections of this study, especially Chapter Nine, have stressed the view that, in Baganda Ntu'ology to be is »to be in relation to«. That means, many relationships that one had before death are nurtured even after his/her death. Hence, the living-dead, too, is a relational being, as he/she continues to participate in the life of his/her basic society. Moreover, the Baganda hold that their society comprises both the living and the living-dead.

There are many forms of nurturing the relationship between the living and the living dead. The words uttered during the mourning rites before one is buried are intended, for instance, to pacify the spirit of the dead. He/she is addressed as if he/she were alive and listening attentively. The dead body is cleansed. In so doing, the living people help their departed friend in order that he/she appears presentable before the other spiritual beings. It is a social ceremony that could be

---

[10] See, also Kyewalyanga, F. X. op. cit., p. 102

likened to the process that a group of friends goes through in helping somebody to dress for a special occasion.

In many Baganda homes one finds a special place which is reserved for the living-dead. In some instances, it is a small and temporary dwelling of simple construction; it is the dwelling of the living dead when they, as it is said, come to visit their living relatives.[11] This is a sign of the unity and relationship that prevails between the particular living and their dead ancestor(s) or relative(s). More so, before drinking, for instance, water, one is supposed to perform an act of unity with the living-dead; it is (pouring) libation, the act pouring a few drops of that liquid as a sacrifice to the living dead.

The bond between the living and the living dead is also strengthened by the rites of installing a heir for the deceased. The heir is in the first place one who succeeds to a hereditary title; he/she may also, or may not be one who inherits or is entitled to inherit property. Through him/her, the living dead is remembered or even honoured by the living.

The popular saying, »*Alifa tazadde, talizuukira*«,[12] demonstrates a strong belief among the Baganda; namely, the belief in the partial re-incarnation of some of the living dead. This is possible, it is held, through the coming into the world of a new-born that bears, actually or potentially, particular hereditary traits that are generally held to be inherited from the particular deceased predecessor. The belief in the partial re-incarnation of some of the living dead is in this way another key element of the relationship between the living and living dead.

The living dead, in Baganda Ntu'ology, are quite concerned about harmony in the universe, to the extent that they are regarded as guardians of the Baganda moral code. It is common belief, therefore, that the living dead intervene time and again to settle matters regarding breaching the moral code.[13]

It is indeed what I have termed »the foreverness of being in relation to« the living dead that has led to given misinterpretations of some elements in Baganda Ntu'ology; e.g. the talk about »ancestor worship«. Such a misinterpretation and wrong portrayal calls for rectifica-

---

[11] For further information on this matter, see, especially, Mpuuga, W. op. cit., 1985, p. 86
[12] Literally, this means: »one who passes away without giving birth to a child will never come back to life.«
[13] Consider, especially: Kyewalyanga, F. X. op. cit., p. 286

tion, since describing »the relationship between Africans and their ancestors as ancestor worship is sentimentally inappropriate, analytically misleading and theoretically unproductive.«[14]

---

[14] Cf. Vchendu, U. C. N. »Igbo Traditional Religion.« in: Africa. Journal of the International Institute of African Languages and Cultures. Vol. 52, No. 21 (1982), p. 100f.

Aspect four
Introducing an African Philosophy?

Various statements of the meaning of words or word groups have guided the course of this study. Consider the subsequent definitions and descriptions that have come up again and again for reference in the antecedent chapters.

Referring to the thought of the Baganda, I defined *wisdom* as: »a corpus of knowledge, naturally acquired and ordered, which in guiding and/or determining the life pattern of the Baganda offers fundamental explanations of things.«

Ntu'ology is wisdom that is the ultimate principle for a classification of reality and values according to NTU categories. *Baganda Ntu'ology* is a Ntu'ology that manifests itself in the gamut of the Baganda myths, beliefs, customs, taboos, rituals and like practices that govern the various patterns of the life of the Baganda and/or determine their view of the world in general, of the human being and of suprahuman beings. *Baganda Ntu'ology* is, therefore, a distinctive Baganda sphere of Ntu'ological thought.

Baganda Ntu'ology is sub-divided into *Wantu'ology, Kintu'ology, Muntu'ology* and *Buntu'ology*. *Wantu'ology, Kintu'ology, Muntu'ology* is wisdom that is the basic principle for a classification of reality and values (in Baganda Ntu'ology) according to the *Wantu, Kintu, Muntu* categories of being, respectively.

Buntu'ology is wisdom that is the basic principle for a classification of reality and values (in Baganda Ntu'ology) according to the modality category or the *Buntu* category of being.

The above given definitions and descriptions present us with a summary of an extended expression of thought on the theme, »Baganda Ntu'ology«. This list of definitions and descriptions is hence a general review of a set of introductory remarks regarding a discourse on Baganda Ntu'ology. In this connection, I shall let this study die at a search for an answer to the following question: Since Baganda Ntu'ology is a type of wisdom, is a discourse on Baganda Ntu'ology a philosophy? This question presupposes a common agreement on a general definition of philosophy; that is: that philosophy is »a discourse on wisdom.«

Chapter eleven
A Discourse on Baganda Ntu'ology

Notwithstanding the urgency for answering the significant question, »Is a discourse on Baganda Ntu'ology a philosophy?« posed above, I intend, in the concluding chapter of this study, to describe the key parameters of a discourse on Baganda Ntu'ology. This endeavour is necessary in providing a background against which the mentioned question may be answered.

Experience: The Source of Baganda Ntu'ology

It is a point of general consent among philosophers that the starting-point of philosophizing is experience.[1] That is, philosophizing begins with the usual conscious perception or apprehension of the reality around us. This »the usual conscious perception or apprehension of reality« is commonly expressed in our »usual« life practices, but most significantly in our »usual« way of expressing thoughts, opinions, or feelings through the spoken word.

In the foregoing summarization of given basic issues relating to *wantu'*ology, *kintu'*ology, *muntu'*ology and *buntu'*ology, I have depended upon myths, beliefs, customs, taboos, rituals, popular epigrams or maxims, etc. for my basic sources of information. Since these sources of information directly or indirectly regard guidelines that give orientation to the various patterns of the life and world-views of the Baganda in general, one may conclude that they are results of the usual conscious perception or apprehension of reality; they are products of the usual conscious perception or apprehension of external, material or non-material events; they are conclusions based upon a direct partici-

---

[1] Consider, for instance, the description of this type of experience *(empeiria)* by Aristotle of Stagira (384–322 B.C.) in his: Metaphysics *(Metaphysica)* I, 1, 980–981a.

pation in events; they are pieces of knowledge, aspects of skills or practice derived from direct observation of or participation in events; they are, in short, products of experience.

In order to demonstrate the way or manner in which »the usual conscious perception or apprehension of reality« may be raw material for philosophy, let us take the general example of the brief popular sayings, epigrams or maxims, i.e., the proverbs quoted in the foregoing sections.

The Luganda word group that is the equivalent of the English term »proverb« is, »*olugero olusonge*«. *Olugero* may be translated as »a measuring stick«. It is a noun derived from the verb »*okugera*«, meaning »to ascertain the measurements of something«, or simply, »to measure«. Understood from this angle, a proverb may be considered as experience which has been regulated by a certain standard, and summarized into a brief popular saying. The message of such a saying, in its turn, becomes a standard by which other or similar life experiences may be measured.

The adjective *olusonge* roots in the verb *okusonga* which means to poke, prod, or pierce. Accordingly, *olusonge* may mean the adjective »sharp or penetrating«. Hence *olugero olusonge* is a proverb, a summary of words of wisdom which are, so to say, sharpened by experience in order to penetrate the minds of those who make use of it, or in order to give direction like a pointed arrow does.

The following definition of *olugero olusonge*, put forward by a person of experience, rhythms well with my foregoing interpretation of a proverb in Luganda. According to Anatoli Wasswa, a proverb is »a group of words bearing a lot of meaning in a summary form, which our ancestors formulated basing themselves upon direct participation in events and situations, words which people may at all times adapt to their life situations.«[2]

What has been said above regarding *olugero olusonge*, the proverb, vis-à-vis »the usual conscious perception or apprehension of reality« as the starting-point of philosophy, applies *mutatis mutandis* to Baganda myths, beliefs, customs, taboos, rituals etc. which I have used as my basic sources of information in the antecedent sections of this work.

---

[2] I have freely translated this definition from the Luganda original work; see Wasswa, A. Gakuweebwa Munno. (An unpublished, undated Essay), p. 2

Wonder: The Outset of Baganda Ntu'ological Questioning

Rapt astonishment at something new to one's experience, admiration for something which appears to be other than anything previously known or anticipated, etc. are good signs of a basic dissatisfaction with our usual environment of experience. The cause of such astonishment or admiration is wonder. Philosophers regard wonder to be the outset of philosophical questioning or questions.[3]

From the Baganda myths, beliefs, customs, taboos, rituals etc. which I employed as my basic sources of information in the antecedent sections of this work, I wish to choose out the taboos, and dwell on the process of instituting a taboo. In so doing, I intend to demonstrate that wonder is for Baganda Ntu'ology, too, the outset of serious questioning or questions.

Let us take the example of the Baganda prohibition for a boy against the intimate touching of the hand of the daughter of his father's or his mother's sister. According the Baganda social-moral customs, one should abstain from such an act for fear of developing a health mal-condition of acting nervously, or for fear of harm from the living dead who are key guardians of the Baganda moral code. From the social biological point of view, however, this type of taboo guards against the possible or eventual undesirable interbreeding of closely related individuals.

The fact that there is in Luganda a word that applies to the act of breaching such a taboo,[4] indicates that some individuals have ever been or are continually curious about, so to speak, challenging the rightness of this taboo. To challenge the rightness of such a taboo is equivalent to exposing oneself to danger beyond what is called for by social duty or courage. To the venturesome persons, who take such a risk, however, is this element of the Baganda moral code either borne out of ignorance, or it is has become outdated.

Such basic dissatisfaction rouses one to question the sense there is in the acts of one's usual environment of experience. This basic dissatisfaction with one's usual environment of experience arouses the cour-

---

[3] It is this type of wonder that Plato or Aristocles (427–347 B.C.) talks about in the Dialogue Theaetetus (Theaitetos) 155d; and so does Aristotle of Stagira (384–322 B.C.) in his: Metaphysics *(Metaphysica)* I, 2, 982b.
[4] The word is, »*ekivve*« and signifies an abominable act of breaching the moral code.

age needed for an undertaking involving danger and unknown risks. The courage to undergo the act of challenging such a taboo is certainly related to an open or silent admiration for something which appears to be other than anything previously known, accepted or anticipated. The underlying cause of such astonishment and admiration is wonder. It is, hence, wonder which rouses one to question the established system; it is wonder that conduces one to admire the unknown alternative.

It is my position that, when wonder rouses critical individuals to question the established social order, society often responds to that situation by devising means of elevating a simple social rule to the level of a social practice which ought to be common to all, i.e. a social custom. How does society realize this?

In my view, society begins by recognizing the fact that the questions of its critical individuals members make sense. Society appropriates these questions, since it realizes the necessity and urgency for change, which the questions of the critical individual members suggest. However, society appropriates these questions in a reticent manner. That is, society shuns any occasion of giving the full measure of credit to the critical individual members whose questions initiated the respective process of change. It eludes any possible notice by the public that the new situation was originally not its (society's) brain child. In this way, while silently embracing the questions of its critical individual members, society publicly elevates a simple social rule to the level of a social custom.

Going back to the above mentioned taboo, I am of the view that what most probably was initiated as a social biological rule against the possible or eventual undesirable interbreeding of closely related individuals, has eventually turned out to be a prohibition imposed by Baganda social customs. Baganda Ntu'ology or Buntu'ology in particular has dressed up this prohibition with socio-moral elements: it is not only a prohibition, but as well a protective measure for the preservation of harmony in the universe. That is, it is a prohibition that has found its rightful place in Buntu'ology.

The rightness of any action that respects that taboo is therefore considered as dependent on or connected with both the goodness or value of that particular action or its consequences to the individual, and the goodness or value of that same action or its consequences to his/her social group.

Doubt: The Rise of Baganda Ntu'ological Critical Views

The basic dissatisfaction with one's usual environment of experience, described above, arouses a feeling of uncertainty about the accepted norms and ways of life in that environment. It excites the inclination not to believe or accept much regarding the established order in the same environment. This is a situation of doubt, of taking a sceptical outlook towards the usual environment of experience. Philosophers generally hold that doubt or the negative inclination not to believe or accept much regarding one's usual environment of experience may breed not only acts of criticising, but also the positive search for fundamental, substitute certainty.[5]

Let us take an example of an issue regarding the highly regarded authority of the elders among the Baganda, an issue discussed in Chapter Eight above. In revisiting this issue, I intend to demonstrate that Baganda Ntu'ology is capable of responding or conforming to changing or new situations; and, in so doing, it gives »doubt« a chance to develop new critical views.

Discussing the ethics of truth and falsehood in *Buntu'ology*, we observed that, in cases where the authority of an elder – authority which binds a family together – is likely to be challenged by means of a message of truth to be delivered by an inferior person, priority is thereby given to the role of authority in binding people, and not to truth when it separates people. This would be done in good faith, and, without the intention to compromise the truth.

We also noted that the relative phrase, »*omukulu tasobya*« (an elder does not err or stray) is, for instance, never used to exhibit how infallible the elders are. But, it is a strong reminder for any younger party who tries to challenge an elder unnecessarily.

These two instances could present *Buntu'ology* or Baganda Ntu'ology as such, as a very rigid system of thought and practice. Relating to the same issue of the authority of the elders, however, one observes that there is room for flexibility, as expressed by the following

---

[5] One is hereby reminded about the young Augustine's sceptical outlook vis-à-vis the possibility of knowing the truth, his inner struggle to search for substitute explanations and eventually, his victory in overcoming this phase. On this matter, see, especially: St. Augustine *(Aurelius Augustinus)*, On the Trinity *(De Trinitate)*, X, 10.

proverb: »*Ne gwozadde akukubira engoma n'ozina*«. That is, »your own child may set for you the tune for the dance.«

In accordance with the Baganda social-human-moral code, the rules governing one's usual environment of experience are set by the elders, beginning with the immediate elders, i.e., one's parents. The proverb, »*Ne gwozadde akukubira engoma n'ozina*«, on the other hand, envisages the possibility of an occasion or occasions, whereby the children fix, decide on, prescribe, set the rules of life, rules which the parents, the elders have to follow.

Like any other *olugero olusonge* or proverb, this proverb is derived from experience, experience which is the source of Baganda NTU'ology, as already observed. The direct message of this proverb concerns the authority of the elders. But the wider meaning that it carries, like all Baganda proverbs do, may be applied to several other occasions of life. The general experience upon which this proverb is based is, therefore, the experience regarding the continual need for flexibility in a variety of matters of human life. That means, specifically, that in times when one has a basic dissatisfaction with one's usual environment of experience, or in times when one has a feeling of uncertainty about the accepted norms and ways of life in that environment, or in times when one feels an inclination not to believe or accept much regarding the same environment, Baganda Ntu'ology allows for the positive search for a fundamental, substitute certainty.

Final Conclusion

The foregoing notes have highlighted three parameters typical of a discourse on Baganda Ntu'ology. They are: experience, wonder and doubt. These three factors form the aspect under which this type of wisdom, which I have named Baganda Ntu'ology, offers fundamental explanations of things; they form the formal object of Baganda Ntu'ology.

Moreover the above described three parameters constitute a foundation upon which any further attempts to answer the question »Is a discourse on Baganda Ntu'ology a philosophy?« may be based.

References

ASHTON E. O., et. al.
  A Luganda Grammar, London: 1954
ANZENBACHER A.
  Einführung in die Philosophie, Freiburg/Basel/Wien: 1999
ARENDT H.
  The Life of the Mind, London: 1978
ARISTOTLE (of Stagira)
  Metaphysica (Metaphysics) I, 1, 980–981a.
ARISTOTLE (of Stagira)
  Metaphysica (Metaphysics) I, 2, 982b.
AUGUSTINUS A.
  De Trinitate (On the Trinity), X, 10.
CHUKWUDI E. E. (ed.)
  African Philosophy: An Anthology, Malden: 1998: pp. 1–55
DDIBA J. L.
  Eddiini mu Buganda, Kitovu: 1955
DEMPWOLF O.
  »Sprachforschung und Mission,« in: Richter D. J., Hrsg.
  Das Buch der deutschen Weltmission, Gotha: 1935
DE RAEYMAEKER L.
  Introduction to Philosophy, New York: 1960
EMEFIE I. M.
  God and Man in African Religion, London: 1981
GBADEGESIN S.
  African Philosophy – Traditional Yoruba Philosophy and Contemporary African Realities, New York: 1991
GYEKYE K.
  An Essay on African Philosophical Thought- The Akan Conceptual Scheme, Cambridge, 1987.
HEIDEGGER M.
  Being and Time, New York: 1962
JAHN J.
  Muntu. The New African Culture, New York: 1961
JAHN J.
  Muntu. Umrisse der neoafrikanischen Kultur, Köln: 1958

References

Kagame A.
La Philosophie Bantu Compareé, Paris: 1976

Kagame A., dt. Übers.
Sprache und Sein: die Ontologie der Bantu Zentralafrikas, Heidelberg: 1985

Kaggwa A.
Ekitabo ky'Empisa z'Abaganda, Kampala: 1918

Kaphagawani D. N.
»What is African Philosophy?« in: P. H. Coetzee and A. P. J. Roux (eds.): The African Philosophy Reader, London: 1998, pp. 86–98

Kawere E. K. N.
Bukadde Magezi, Nairobi: 1968

Kimmerle H.
Philosophie in Afrika – afrikanische Philosophie, Frankfurt am Main: 1991

Kyewalyanga F. X.
Traditional Religion, Customs, and Christianity in Uganda, Freiburg im Breisgau: 1976

Lugira A. M.
Ganda Art. Kampala: 1970

Marsh Z.
An Introduction to the History of East Africa, Kingsnorth G. W., London/Cambridge: 1957

Maurier H.
»Do we have an African Philosophy?« in: Wright A. R. African Philosophy: An Introduction, Washington D.C.: 1974

Mbiti J. S.
African Religions and Philosophy, Bungay Suffolk: 1985

Mbiti J. S.
Concepts of God in Africa, London/New York: 1970

Mbiti J. S.
Introduction to African Religion, London: 1978

Mpuuga W.
Amagezi g'Abedda, Kampala: 1976

Mutaawe K. F.
The Ganda Traditional Law Court Processes and Syllogistic Inference (Unpublished Essay), Katigondo: 1983

Mutaawe K. F.
Self and Social Reality in a Philosophical Anthropology, Frankfurt am Main: 1998

Nevins A. J.
The World Book of Peoples, Huntigton: 1973

Nsimbi B. M.
Amannya Amaganda n'Ennono zaago, Kampala: 1956

Oluoch S. I.
An Introduction to African Philosophy, Lanham, 1998: pp. 8–46

Parrinder G.
Africa's Three Religions, London: 1969

References

PLATO (Aristocles)
  Theaitetos (Theaetetus) 155d
RADCLIFFE B., et al., ed.
  African Systems of Kinship and Marriage, London: 1975
ROSCOE J.
  The Baganda, London: 1965
RUCH E. A./
  African Philosophy. An Introduction to the Main ANYANWU K. C.
  Philosophical Trends in Contemporary Africa, Rome: 1981
SELIGMAN C. G.
  Les Races de L'Afrique, Paris/Payot: 1935
SHORTER A.
  East African Societies, London: 1974
SSEMOGERERE T. M. ed.
  Katekismu ya Mapeera, Kampala: 1983
TEMPELS P.
  Bantu Philosophy, Paris: 1959
TOKUMBOH A.
  Salvation in African Tradition, Nairobi: 1979
VCHENDU U. C. N.
  »Igbo Traditional Religion.« in: Africa. Journal of the International Institute of African Languages and Cultures. Vol. 52, No. 21 (1982), p. 100f
VON KIENLE R.
  Keysers Fremwörterlexikon, Heidelberg/München: 1959
WAHRIG G. et al.
  Deutsches Wörterbuch. München, 1986
WALIGGO J. M.
  »Incarnating Christianity in Uganda,« in: Proceedings of the Second National Theological Week, Katigondo: 1983
WALLACE W. A.
  Elements of Philosophy, New York: 1977
WALSER F.
  Luganda Proverbs, Berlin: 1982
WEBSTER'S
  New Collegiate Dictionary, Springfield/Massachusetts: 1977
WERNER A.
  Structure and Relationships of African Languages, London: 1930
WIREDU K.
  »On Defining African Philosophy«, In: Tsenay Serequeberhan (ed.), African Philosophy: The Essential Readings, New York, 1991: pp. 87–110

Appendix

Epilogue by
Professor Dr. Paul Eisenkopf

Ntu'ology appears at first sight to be a foreign, mechanically coined term. It is indeed a word that the author has created. He even succeeds in both elaborating this new word, and in imparting substance on it.

The linguistic basic root NTU, found in many East and Central African languages, is quite central to this work. NTU could be compared with the Western Philosophy notion of being. NTU is, however, not to be identified with »being«. More so, this linguistic basic root lacks the status of a word. It may only be meaningfully analysed through adding to it an initial vowel, prefix, suffix, etc.; a good example hereby is the word ›Bantu‹, meaning human beings.

Beyond focussing attention on African Philosophy in general, the study centres on the teachings of ancient thinkers of the ethnic group called the Baganda of Southern Uganda.

The linguistic basic root NTU, which not only presents itself as a logical reality that exists in the mind but also offers an intuition into »what is real«, manifests itself four categories of being: Muntu – the category of human beings; Kintu – the category of non-human beings; Wantu – the categories of space and time; and, Buntu -the modality category.

A closer analysis of these categories of being demonstrates the dynamic, anthropocentric approach of the particular world view of the Baganda. Thus, the author considers it to be a »muntu-centric« (anthropocentric) approach. Accordingly, non-human beings are reflected on from a human-being's perspective. While some of these beings form the supra-human world, the goal human life, other non-human beings are thought about as beings that are below the human level and thus as beings under the responsibility of the human being. More so, the categories of time and space and the modality category are interpreted in terms of their relation to the human being.

An additional core point is the meaning of »to be a human being«;

that is,»being in relation to …« Aspect Two of this work centres upon highlighting this philosophical, anthological concept in a variety of ways.

The author succeeds in presenting well the traditional teachings of the Baganda. Thus, by following the elegantly clear language and the orderly presentation of ideas in this work, any Central European reader may find it easy to comprehend this African system of thought.

It is also a noteworthy point that this study is given a firm theoretical base through the frequent use of both the Baganda experience of reality and of their proverbs, which are looked upon as compendia of knowledge.

Another useful tool that guides the reader of this essay is created by the brief words of introduction that open each chapter.

Consequently, this academic piece of work could become the desired key to a meeting point between Western and African philosophical thought. At this point, the closest theoretical connection appears to exist between Baganda and Biblical Hebrew systems of thought. Another clear example is the link between the contents of Chapter Eight that deals with »Muntu-muntu relationship« and Martin Buber's conception of the human being as a »being in dialogue and relationship with other human beings«. In view of that, a dialogue between the Bible and Ntu'ology could bear much fruit.

The study ends with an open-ended question on whether a discourse about Baganda Ntu'ology is a philosophy. The author nevertheless correctly points to the fact he has at least laid the background upon which an answer to that enquiry may be sought.

Prof. Dr. Paul Eisenkopf
Lehrstuhl für Fundamentaltheologie
Phil.-Theol. Hochschule Vallendar
Vallendar, 5.11.2000